The Purpose
and Power of
Praise & Worship

Dr. Myles Munroe

Destiny Image® Publishers, Inc.
P.O. Box 310
Shippensburg, PA 17257-0310

"Speaking to the Purposes of God for This Generation
and for the Generations to Come"

ISBN 0-7684-2047-4

For Worldwide Distribution
Printed in the U.S.A.

This book and all other Destiny Image, Revival Press, Mercy Place, Fresh Bread, and Treasure House books are available at Christian bookstores and distributors worldwide.

For a U.S. bookstore nearest you, call **1-800-722-6774**.
For more information on foreign distributors, call **717-532-3040**.
Or reach us on the Internet: **http://www.reapernet.com**

713 956- 8892

Provider (Gerlinda) ✓
Bi weekly ☒

Texas Home Health

cifate - 6 Weeks shte pood
Brenda cel
Jean

The Purpose
and Power of

Praise & Worship

Bisho Harh →

3683 ced Lex Rd
Winston-Salem NC 27107
Listing side of prayer →

OKPAYMe . com

Dedication

To the human heart that struggles to find the joy, fulfillment, and satisfaction of God's presence.

To all those believers who desire to experience a deeper reality of the awesome presence in their daily life, and to know the joy of taking His presence into the world of family, the world of work, the world of sports, and the world of life.

To my late mother, Evangelist Princess Louise Munroe, my first worship and praise teacher, who is now praising Him among the heavenly host of witnesses.

To Dr. Fuchsia Pickett, a mother in Zion and a true worshiper, who taught me the value of His presence and the intimacy of His love.

To the late Dr. Sam Sasser, who laid the foundation for my understanding of praise and worship with his life, dedication, teaching, and example. Today I know you praise Him in perfection, Sam. May your legacy be ever established by your heart of pure praise and worship.

To Dr. Judson Cornwall, a man of great wisdom and understanding, whose life, ministry, and teaching have been an altar on which the fires of worship and praise have burned for decades. Thanks for the gift of your life.

To Mark Bethel, an outstanding minister of praise and worship, whose dedication, passion, and love for God's presence stands as an inspiring role model for many. May you always lead others into His presence.

To the faithful support of the worship team at Bahamas Faith Ministries, especially Beverley Dwyer, Charles and Ruth Brown, Lionel Harris, Richard Rahamming, and Crystal Worrell. Continue to lead others into His courts of worship.

Acknowledgments

This work is a result of many years as a student at the feet of many teachers and gifted minds. I am forever grateful for the inspiration, wisdom, and example of many great men and women who, through their commitment and passion for His presence, have taught me how to love Him also.

I am also grateful for the members and friends of Bahamas Ministries International Fellowship, whose faithful prayers, support, loyalty, and submission allowed me to develop the principles and thoughts in this work.

For the development and production of this book, I feel a deep sense of gratitude to:

—My wonderful wife, Ruth, and our children, Chairo and Charisa, for their patience, understanding, and support over the years. You make it easy to fulfill God's will.

—Kathy Miller, my gifted and diligent transcriber, editor, and advisor, who again labored with me to bring this work to life. Your ability to capture the essence of my heart and mind is a work of Providence.

—Elizabeth Allen, for her unwavering support and patient pursuit of me in my busy travel schedule to meet deadlines.

—And finally, the object, subject, and purpose of my praise and worship, the only One we should worship, the Omnipotent Father and the Lord Jesus Christ, His manifested presence in flesh, and Holy Spirit.

Endorsements

It is evident that in every new Kairos (special timing of God) He raises up a voice to speak forth, in greater clarity, His predestined purposes and plans for that hour. There is no question in my mind that Dr. Myles Munroe has been raised up for this momentous hour as a voice to the nations as well as to his own precious Bahamas.

Other writers have written well on the subject of praise. I believe Dr. Munroe's work, *The Purpose and Power of Praise & Worship*, will lead the reader into a broader, deeper understanding of God's purpose for praise and worship, and then further into a deeper experiential reality of our privilege to commune with our God in His throne room, not only in Heaven, but bowed before Him at the throne of our hearts.

Dr. Fuchsia T. Pickett
Bible teacher, author
Blountville, Tennessee

In this book, *The Purpose and Power of Praise & Worship*, Myles Munroe offers a fresh stream of understanding the heart of God as it relates to His children. Dr. Munroe feels that praise does not lift us to God's throne; it prepares a place for God to descend to be with us. Adam never ascended to God's throne; God descended to Adam's garden. Those who know the ministry of Dr. Munroe will hear him on every page, and that hearing will bring a freshness to their lives.

Dr. Judson Cornwall
Phoenix, Arizona

Myles Munroe is an anointed teacher with a passion for encouraging and instructing the Body of Christ. In *The Purpose and Power of Praise & Worship*, he reaffirms God's eternal purpose to dwell in the midst of His people and teaches how to invite God's presence into our life. This teaching is crucial for all who hunger to live within the veil, there to find the One for whom their heart longs. Truly, this book will challenge you to seek God through praise and to maintain the conditions that encourage His nearness.

Don Nori
Publisher
Destiny Image, Inc.

Contents

Foreword

From the third chapter of Genesis to the end of the Book of the Revelation, we find God trying to get His people back to the intimate relationship He had with Adam and Eve in the beginning. Because God is holy, perfect and pure, it is impossible for man, who has been conceived in iniquity since the fall of Adam and Eve, to stand in the presence of God without an atonement.

God gave Moses the plan for allowing Himself to dwell in the presence of His people through the building of the ark of God and the tabernacle of God. Through these rituals and sacrifices prescribed by God, the high priest was able to come into the presence of the Almighty and represent the people.

However, through King David, God shows us He desires more than just the blood and sacrifice of selected animals; He desires a pure and contrite heart. Jesus, in His dialogue with the Samaritan woman, tells us that God is looking for worshipers who will worship Him in spirit and truth.

When Jesus taught the disciples the Lord's prayer, He said "...Thy will be done on earth as it is in Heaven...." In the heavenly experience of Isaiah in the sixth chapter of the Book of Isaiah, and

❖ The Purpose and Power of *Praise & Worship*

John in the Revelation, we see what is being done in heaven continually: *praise* and *worship*.

Praise and worship has always been the avenue into the presence of our God. We can talk about Him, do things for Him, and even pray to Him, but it is only through praise and worship that we are allowed to be in the presence of our Great Creator.

In this book, my brother in Christ, my friend and confidant, Myles Munroe, teaches us:

How to praise and worship
Whom to praise and worship
Where to praise and worship
When to praise and worship
The **power** of praise and worship
The patterns of praise and worship
The principles of praise and worship
The practicals of praise and worship
The **purpose** of praise and worship

This book is a must read for those who have a passion to know the heart of God. I prophesy and predict that it will become required or recommended reading in many Christian schools, colleges, universities, and for Bible students throughout the world.

I am honored to make this small contribution to this book. I believe this book is going to be a special blessing to those who desire to live in the awesome presence of our magnificent God.

Dr. Ron Kenoly
World renowned worship leader

Introduction

"God came near. I know He was right there with me." What wonderful words! What a glorious experience! Sadly such experiences come all too infrequently to most of us. Yet life without God's presence was not His original plan for us. He designed us to know Him, living in close, intimate fellowship with Him. That's why life is so difficult and unfulfilling for so many people. We are living without the one thing that is essential for our fulfillment and well-being. We are living without the continuous, enduring presence of God.

> **You were created to live in God's presence. Life anywhere else is a distorted, dissatisfying imitation.**

Whenever you live without a vital, ongoing relationship with God, you have no hope of finding true happiness or of fulfilling the purpose for which you were born. You simply cannot function properly and effectively outside the environment of God's presence.

The purpose of this book is to teach you the conditions under which God's presence draws near to us. For you see, God's presence is conditional. He doesn't come simply because we want Him to. He comes when the conditions are right. Only as we learn to establish and maintain the conditions that He has ordained for His coming can we hope to know the joy of living in His presence on a daily, moment-by-moment basis.

So read and study this book until the principles and truths taught here become a natural part of your thinking. Allow them to equip and inspire you to create the conditions in your life that will welcome the presence of the Lord Jesus Christ and of His Holy Spirit. Then you will grow and flourish, finding the joy and fulfillment that only life in the presence of Almighty God can bring.

Chapter 1

God's Original Plan for Mankind

God's greatest desire as revealed in the Scriptures is for a family.

"In the beginning God created the heavens and the earth" (Gen. 1:1). Land and seas, plants and animals, birds and sea creatures all came forth at His spoken word.

Then God said, "Let Us make man in Our image, in Our likeness, and let them rule over the fish of the sea and the birds of the air, over the livestock, over all the earth, and over all the creatures that move along the ground." So God created man in His own image, in the image of God He created him; male and female He created them. God blessed them and said to them, "Be fruitful and increase in number; fill the earth and subdue it. Rule over the fish of the sea and the birds of the

air and over every living creature that moves on the ground" (Genesis 1:26-28).

This crowning act of creation was a result of God's desire to have a family. He wanted someone to be His friend and to live with Him as a son. God's original plan was that man would share in His authority and rule, not serve Him as a servant. This is why Jesus Christ is the "King of kings and Lord of lords" (Rev. 19:16b), not the King of subjects. God was interested in a completely different kind of relationship than we normally think of when we talk about a king. He wanted sons who would not only be led by the King but who would also exercise the King's authority and rule on earth.

This relationship between God and man is of paramount importance to God. Creation shows this to be true. The first thing God gave man was His image and likeness because that was the first thing God wanted man to have. The second thing God did was to place man in His presence, which is the meaning in the Hebrew language of the word *Eden*. Therefore, God's greatest desire was that man would act like Him and live with Him.

> **G**od wanted man to have His image and likeness and to live in His presence.

The word *image* means "resemblance" (Strong's, H6754) or "exact likeness" (Webster's, "image"). Therefore, to be made in God's image means that man resembles God and is an exact likeness of Him. He has God's true nature and His spiritual and moral character. In the Scriptures, the word *Eden* refers to a place of God's presence (see Is. 51:3; Ezek. 28:13). So God gave man His nature and then put Him in His presence. These were God's priorities.

God did not establish reverent patterns, pious traditions, or religious activities in the Garden of Eden. There was simply a relationship between God and man. Establishing and maintaining this relationship continues to be God's primary concern. He is much more concerned about our fellowship with Him than about our works, our activities, our traditions, and even our busyness. God wants relationship—that's the bottom line—and everything God established for man was built on this desire for fellowship.

Thus, God created man for a specific purpose: to have dominion over all the earth; with an image different from that of all other parts of His creation: His own spiritual and moral nature; and with the ability to function like He does: seeing things that are not yet visible (faith). The Scriptures clearly show this intent of God that man would be more like Him than the rest of creation, and that he would think and act like God.

> **What is man that You are mindful of him, the son of man that You care for him? You made him a little lower than the heavenly beings and crowned him with glory and honor. You made him ruler over the works of Your hands; You put everything under his feet** (Psalm 8:4-6; see also Hebrews 2:6-8).

Truly, the creation of man was God's greatest production, and He described the man He had made as being "very good" (see Gen. 1:31). Sadly, what God intended for man and man's current experience are quite different. This difference is a result of man's choice to disregard the principles that are an inherent part of God's creation.

God Is a God of Principles

Man's ability to fulfill his purpose and to be all God intended him to be is predicated on the requirement that he obey the principles God established when He created human beings. Why is this true? God is a God of principles. Everything He created was established to operate by certain principles that guarantee its proper function. This pattern in creation includes human beings. We were created to operate by principles that God established before He created us.

These principles or rules of operation for human beings are found throughout the Bible, although they are not always referred to as principles. They may also be referred to as God's laws, ordinances, precepts, statutes, commands, commandments, decrees, instructions, word, and ways. Although the meaning of each of these words carries a slightly different nuance from the others, they all carry within them the basic concept of a principle, which is a law that is established to preserve and protect a created thing and to assure its maximum performance. So each time these words occur in Scripture, the particular word used may be removed and the word *principle* may be inserted in its place. These varying words for God's principles can be clearly seen in Psalms 19 and 119:

> **The law [principles] of the Lord is perfect, reviving the soul. The statutes [principles] of the Lord are trustworthy, making wise the simple. The precepts [principles] of the Lord are right, giving joy to the heart. The commands [principles] of the Lord are radiant, giving light to the eyes. The fear of the Lord is pure, enduring forever. The ordinances [principles] of the Lord are sure and altogether righteous. They are more precious than gold, than much pure gold; they are sweeter than honey, than honey from the comb. By them is Your servant warned; in keeping them there is great reward (Psalm 19:7-11).**

> **Blessed are they whose ways are blameless, who walk according to the law [principles] of the Lord. Blessed are they who keep His statutes [principles] and seek Him with all their heart. They do nothing wrong; they walk in His ways [principles]. You have laid down precepts [principles] that are to be fully obeyed. Oh, that my ways were steadfast in obeying Your decrees [principles]! Then I would not be put to shame when I consider all Your commands [principles]. I will praise You with an upright heart as I learn Your righteous laws [principles]. I will**

obey Your decrees [principles]; do not utterly forsake me. How can a young man keep his way pure? By living according to Your word [principles]. I seek You with all my heart; do not let me stray from Your commands [principles]. I have hidden Your word [principles] in my heart that I might not sin against You. Praise be to You, O Lord; teach me Your decrees [principles]. With my lips I recount all the laws [principles] that come from Your mouth. I rejoice in following Your statutes [principles] as one rejoices in great riches. I meditate on Your precepts [principles] and consider Your ways [principles]. I delight in Your decrees [principles]; I will not neglect Your word [principles]. Do good to Your servant, and I will live; I will obey Your word [principles]. Open my eyes that I may see wonderful things in Your law [principles] (Psalm 119:1-18).

Characteristics of Principles

Since a satisfying relationship with God, each other, and the rest of God's creation is predicated on our obeying His principles in creation, let's look now at some of the characteristics or properties of principles. Understanding these properties can help us to understand how principles function in our life.

- *Principles are permanent.* When God created human beings, He created them to breathe oxygen. Although many years have passed since God first formed man from the dust of the earth, and man has found many ways to "better" his life experience, man still needs oxygen to survive. In essence, any environment where oxygen is absent is deadly to man.

- *Principles never change; they remain constant.* In the English system of measurement, a yard has been determined to equal 36 inches. Now you may create a stick that measures 35 inches long and call it a "yardstick," but this in no way changes the principle that a yard is a unit of measurement equal in length to the sum of 36 inches. In essence, a stick 35 inches in length is not equal to a yard no matter what you call it, because a yard, by the principles of its definition, contains 36 inches. In a similar manner, modifications by our society to God's standards of conduct do not change God's law. God's law is constant, even as He is constant (see Num. 23:19).

- *Principles work anywhere.* One of the laws of nature is that water freezes at 32 degrees Fahrenheit (or 0 degrees Celsius). It doesn't matter whether you freeze water at the north pole or at the equator, water cooled to 32 degrees F (assuming the water is not contaminated with other substances that skew the water's freezing point) will turn to ice. In the same manner, we can expect that God's laws apply to us no matter where or when we live. His principles are applicable in all times, cultures, and geographic locations.

- *Principles protect the product.* This characteristic of principles can be illustrated by the care labels that many clothing manufacturers sew into their garments at the collar or a side seam. These specifications by the manufacturer regarding the garment's care may include requirements concerning water temperature for washing, line drying versus the use of a clothes dryer, and washing in water versus dry cleaning. The manufacturer provides these instructions to protect the clothing from possible harm that could result in shrinkage of the fabric, color loss, premature breakdown of the fibers, or other damage. God's laws are also intended to protect us from harm. Although they may at times appear to limit our choices, these limitations are always given by God to protect our freedom and well-being.

- *Principles can never be broken.* The laws of gravity state that the mass of the earth, the moon, or another planet will exert a certain pull on objects at or near its surface. This pull will draw the objects toward it. With the invention of airplanes, helicopters, and other modes of air transportation, one might say that the laws of gravity have been broken. Such a statement can never be true because a principle of creation cannot be broken. What can happen is that man devises various means to combat or redirect the forces of gravity. Then, although the principle of gravity is not evident in a particular event or circumstance, the principle itself—that is, the rule that objects at or near the earth's surface are pulled toward the earth if they are not in some manner prevented from doing so—still holds true.

- *Principles, when violated, produce destruction.* What seems right to you for the use of a product is not necessarily in agreement with what the manufacturer of a product intended. For example, when you buy an iron, the box it comes in contains a little booklet that lists the commandments or laws of the manufacturer concerning its function. These are often called the operating instructions. They tell you how to use the iron so you get the maximum performance from it.

Now you could take that iron, plug it into the wall, and put it into the bathtub with you to heat up the water. Since an iron is supposed to get hot, that way may seem right to you: "The iron is hot and the water is cold, so I'll just put the iron into the water to make it warm." Guess what? There's a way that seems right unto a man, but the end of it is a shocking experience!

Both you and the iron will suffer damage because of your choice to violate the iron's operating instructions (principles).

- *Principles contain inherent judgment.* This last characteristic of principles is particularly important. For example, the principle of fire is heat. When you put your hand in fire, you can expect to get burned because fire produces heat. In other words, you don't get burned because God burns you or the devil burns you. You get burned because heat is a principle of fire. In essence, the judgment—the burn—is inherent in the principle.

Thus, much of what we call "acts of God" are simply judgments that are inherent in God's principles of creation. For example, God has killed no man. Rather, "the wages [natural results] of sin is death" (Rom. 6:23a). When you play around with sin and start flirting with things you shouldn't be doing, you don't have to worry whether someone will find you out because your own activities will tell on you. Why is this true? Sin contains an inherent judgment. When you violate God's principle, the principle itself contains your discipline or punishment.

God's Use of Principles

The verses previously quoted from Psalms 19 and 119 also clearly reveal the necessity of understanding and obeying God's principles of creation. This is true because only the manufacturer of a product knows what factors are necessary to obtain the maximum operation of the product. In essence, you can't use a product according to your own ideas and expect it to fulfill what the manufacturer promised it could and would do. If you want a product to work, doing all that the manufacturer said it would do, you have to obey the principles (laws, commandments, instructions, etc.) of the one who designed and made the product.

God's demands of us are always based on His principles because He knows we cannot fulfill our purpose and enjoy fulfillment in life unless we operate within the parameters (principles) He has set for us. The effects of His laws cannot be avoided because they are inherent to the law. Therefore, our relationship with God, both our perception of Him and His response to us, is based on how we respond to the principles He has established throughout creation. He is not capricious in His responses to us, but rather is faithful and just. (See Psalm 111:7 and First John 1:9.)

> **I**f you want a product to work, you have to obey the manufacturer's principles of operation.

We may prefer lawlessness, which is the freedom to do whatever we want to do, but our very creation by God, our Manufacturer and Source, requires that we follow His principles. Should we choose lawlessness—doing what we want, when we want, how we want—we can expect to reap the inevitable results, which include slavery, death, and the loss of privileges or freedoms. This is precisely what happened to the man and the woman in the Garden of Eden.

Disregard for God's Principles Carries Consequences

When God placed the man in Eden, He gave him some instructions that were to govern his life in the garden. One of these instructions concerned what he could and could not eat.

> **And the Lord God commanded the man, "You are free to eat from any tree in the garden; but you must not eat from the tree of the knowledge of good and evil, for when you eat of it you will surely die"** (Genesis 2:16-17).

Please note that this command contains an inherent judgment. Death is the proscribed consequence for disobeying this principle.

Thus, God's pronouncement to the man in Genesis 3:19—"By the sweat of your brow you will eat your food until you return to the ground, since from it you were taken; for dust you are and *to dust you will return*"—is nothing more than the logical consequence of man's choice to disobey God.

This physical death that will inevitably claim every person, whether in infancy or in old age, is not, however, the only death man suffered because of his disobedience. The more serious consequence of man's disregard for God's principles for life in the garden was his loss of the Holy Spirit and his subsequent separation from God. This spiritual death, as it may be called, is at the root of all the ills that plague us as individuals and as a society. In truth, man cannot and will not live up to the potential and purpose God built into him until the love and intimacy God and man enjoyed in the garden is restored. Because life in the presence of God is man's ideal environment, God's presence is also his greatest need. Man cannot truly live until the relationship between God and man is restored.

> **D**eath is the absence of the presence of God in a man or a woman's life.

❖ **PRINCIPLES** ❖

1. God created man to share His image and authority.

2. God is more interested in relationship than in rules and traditions.

3. Everything God created is governed by principles.

4. Fulfillment of purpose requires obeying God's principles.

5. Principles contain these inherent characteristics:

    - Principles are permanent.

    - Principles never change.

    - Principles work anywhere.

    - Principles protect the product.

    - Principles can never be broken.

    - Principles, when violated, produce destruction.

    - Principles contain inherent judgment.

6. God's Word contains the principles that govern men and women.

7. Disobeying God's commandments brings natural and spiritual consequences.

Chapter 2

Man's Greatest Need

**God's greatest desire and man's
deepest need is to share an enduring,
Spirit-to-spirit relationship.**

Since God is a God of principles, everything He created was established to operate by certain principles that guarantee its proper function. So all created things—whether plant, animal, fish, bird, star, or human being—must adhere to the principles that govern their life if they are to release their potential and fulfill their purpose. One of the most important of these principles ordained by God to preserve and protect His handiwork and to assure the maximum performance of each created thing is the principle of environment.

The Principle of Environment

The word *environment* is defined as "circumstances, objects, and conditions by which one is surrounded" (Webster's, "environment").

Therefore, an environment may refer to the forces that affect the state of things, the components that make up the climate in which something exists, or the conditions in which a thing exists. Everything in life was created to function within the particular environment that God prescribed for it before He created it.

In essence, before the moment of creation, God decided both what He would make His creation from and where He would place it after He had made it. This place designed to individually suit the makeup and purpose of each thing God made was its environment. When the environment was ready, God called forth each creation from its intended source and put it in the specific environment He had made for it.

So before God created the sun and the moon and the myriad of stars, He first called forth the light and separated it from the darkness, calling the light "day" and the darkness "night." He also made a firmament or expanse to separate the waters above from the waters below and called the firmament "sky." Only then, after all this was completed, did God call forth the lights from the heavens and set them in the sky to mark the day, the night, and the seasons. (See Genesis 1:1-8,14-18.)

God's process in creating plants and animals reveals the same pattern. Before He spoke plants and animals into being, He gathered the waters together so that dry ground would appear. The dry ground He called "land" and the waters He called "seas." Only then did He speak to the sea, commanding it to bring forth the many kinds of fish and sea creatures, and to the land, commanding it to bring forth all manner of vegetation, seed-bearing plants and trees according to their kind, and all living creatures, livestock and wild animals according to their kind. (See Genesis 1:9-12,20-25.)

Finally, God was ready to make man.

Then God said, "Let Us make man in Our image, in Our likeness, and let them rule over the fish of the sea and the birds of the air, over the livestock, over all the

earth, and over all the creatures that move along the ground." So God created man in His own image, in the image of God He created him; male and female He created them (Genesis 1:26-27).

These verses from Genesis clearly reveal that God is man's source. When God made man, He spoke to Himself and man came out of Him. Thus, man was created both to be of the same essence as God, who is spirit (see Jn. 4:24), and to live in the same environment as God, which is the realm of the spirit or the environment of God.

So we see that God prescribed an environment for everything He created before He created it. Then He placed the thing in it.[1] Therefore, you cannot expect one of God's products to function properly if you do not understand the environment He prescribed for it. In essence, a misplaced product will malfunction if you do not follow the prescription for the environment God ordained. A product in the wrong environment just won't work properly.

God prescribed an environment for everything He created. Therefore, environments can be good or bad, positive or negative, healthy or unhealthy depending on what the manufacturer prescribed for the product you are using. The environment itself is not necessarily bad, negative, or unhealthy. Rather the problem is a misplaced product. A particular environment is wrong only because the product was not designed to function in it. The prescription and the actuality don't match.

---

1. The New International Version of the Bible is one of the few versions to use the past perfect "had planted" in Genesis 2:8 concerning God's planting of the Garden of Eden. Most versions simply use the past tense "planted," and some versions even begin verse 8 with the word "then," which would seem to indicate that God planted the garden after He created man. In either case, it is clear that God took great care in creating man's ideal environment. The order of creation does not change the fact that God planned man's ideal environment before He created him. God planned that He was to be man's source and environment, so He spoke to Himself when He created man.

To say it another way, the nature of the environment will always affect the state, function, and efficiency of a product. If, for example, you buy a $5,000 television, throw it into the ocean, then try to make it work, you will soon find that you wasted your $5,000. Or, if you drag a boat down a highway behind a truck, you will find when you try to use the boat in the water that it has been destroyed by the road. Why has this happened? You put the television and the boat into the wrong environment. The manufacturer never intended that you would put the television into the ocean or drag the boat on the highway.

Therefore, no matter how expensive the product is, it will shut down if the environment of operation is different from what the manufacturer intended. A wrong environment—that is, an environment where the product is out of place—will always translate into wasted potential. Truly the key to a product's efficient and effective operation is the environment in which it is placed.

Consequently, we must clearly understand the environment prescribed for each product because it is the environment that determines the product's success or failure. This prescribed environment is what we may call a product's ideal environment. An ideal environment means that there is a perfect environment that God (or a manufacturer) has prescribed for each product. This is why God placed the man in Eden. Eden is man's ideal environment.

Man's Ideal Environment

When God planned what man would be (spirit) and how man would function (by faith), He also determined where man would live (his ideal environment). God didn't take the man and put him just anywhere on earth. God chose a specific spot on this big planet and put the man in that specially chosen place, which we know as Eden. Now let's try to figure out what Eden is.

The root in Hebrew of the word *Eden* is uncertain. The Greek version of the Old Testament, the Septuagint, relates the word to the Hebrew verb *eden* or *ayden*, which means "delight" (Strong's, H5731, H5730). Therefore, *Eden* is translated as the garden of delight. Other occurrences of the word *Eden* in the Old Testament equate *Eden* with the garden of the Lord.

> **The Lord will surely comfort Zion and will look with compassion on all her ruins; He will make her deserts like Eden, her wastelands like the garden of the Lord. Joy and gladness will be found in her, thanksgiving and the sound of singing** (Isaiah 51:3).

> **You were in Eden, the garden of God...** (Ezekiel 28:13).

This seems to concur with the Genesis description of the garden as the place where God walked in the cool of the day (see Gen. 3:8).

Thus, God prepared a garden for man, an environment where it was pleasant and where His presence touched earth. This is why the Bible never says that Adam planted the garden. Rather, God was the One who planted the garden. That is, God came and impressed (planted) His presence in the earth.

Can you get a picture of this? Eden was the one place where God's presence dwelt on earth. It was the garden of His presence, the spot of His pleasantness, and that was precisely where God placed Adam. Unbroken fellowship between God and man was the environment that God planned for man.

This means that you don't need church services, choirs, worship services, and meetings to succeed in life. There were none of these in Eden. Neither were there prophets, teachers, preachers, or apostles. Your ideal environment is nothing more and nothing less than the presence of God Himself, which was God's first gift to Adam.

God's presence is your ideal environment.

His presence in your house is the most beautiful presence in the world. You don't need a husband or a wife to succeed. You need the presence of God. Consequently,

God gave Adam Himself before He gave him a woman. The first presence you need is a God-friend, not a boyfriend or a girlfriend. If you get a boyfriend or girlfriend, a husband or a wife, outside of God's presence, you have created a state of malfunction for yourself.

Why is this true? Everything that is not in its ideal environment malfunctions. This is inevitable. No person or product can function properly outside the environment specifically designed for it by its manufacturer. So just as fish have to stay in water and plants have to stay in the ground if they are to flourish, so man must stay in God's presence. Any fish that removes itself from water or is removed by another creature will eventually die and rot. The same is true of a plant. No plant can continue to live and bear fruit if its roots are not covered and nourished by the ground. In truth, a plant starts to die the instant its roots are removed from the ground, and its death is certain unless its roots are returned to the soil that is its source and ideal environment. Likewise, man's life and the fulfillment of his destiny are possible only to the extent that he walks and talks with God in the garden of His presence.

Man's Fall From God's Presence

Sadly, what God intended and the reality of man's situation today are quite different. The reason for this difference is man's choice to throw off what he perceived to be the restrictive principles of God's design. The fall of man, as man's choice to sin is often called, is really a fall from God's presence, with the accompanying loss of the Holy Spirit. Since God created man to live in relationship with Him and sin caused a breach in that relationship, man's opportunity to live in God's presence ended. The Book of Genesis describes it this way:

So the Lord God banished him from the Garden of Eden to work the ground from which he had been taken. After He drove the man out, He placed on the east side of the Garden of Eden cherubim and a flaming sword

flashing back and forth to guard the way to the tree of life (Genesis 3:23-24).

Since, as we previously noted, the word *Eden* in the Scriptures means the place of God's presence, man's banishment from Eden meant banishment from God's presence. The creature God had created to live in His presence was condemned to live apart from the One who was essential to His well-being. Human history shows the consequences of that separation, consequences that were built into God's principles for man's life.

Now we have to work hard to get into God's presence; but that was not what God intended for the human beings He had created. We were supposed to wake up every morning and go walking in the bush with God. We weren't supposed to have to work ourselves up with singing, instruments, and worship calisthenics to get us into the right mood or frame of mind for worship. God's intent was that we would wake up in His presence, go to sleep in His presence, work in His presence, talk in His presence, go fishing in His presence, eat in His presence, cry in His presence, laugh in His presence, dance in His presence, and on and on. Every part of our life was to be done within the presence of God.

Oh, how we've fallen. What was once our God-given privilege is now denied us by God Himself. For when God sent the man and the woman away from Eden, from the place or moment of His presence, He also set cherubim at the entrance to the garden to be sure that mankind would not return to the environment that had been his home before his sin.

Why would God, who loves man and who created him to live in fellowship with Him, do this? Why would He banish man from His presence and ensure that he could not return? Might it be that the presence of God was so important God would not allow it to be contaminated by man's sin? Might it be that man could no longer endure the presence of God because he had lost the Holy

Spirit, that which enabled him to communicate with God and to enjoy fellowship with Him?

God Is Holy

The Scriptures clearly state that God is holy, which means that God is completely pure in motive and perfect in goodness, righteousness, and justice.

> **Exalt the Lord our God and worship at His holy mountain, for the Lord our God is holy** (Psalm 99:9).

> **The Lord Almighty is the One you are to regard as holy, He is the One you are to fear...** (Isaiah 8:13).

> **For your Maker is your husband—the Lord Almighty is His name—the Holy One of Israel is your Redeemer; He is called the God of all the earth** (Isaiah 54:5).

> **But the Lord Almighty will be exalted by His justice, and the holy God will show Himself holy by His righteousness** (Isaiah 5:16).

Not only is God holy, He is "most" holy in that no other god, person, or thing is as holy as He is (see 1 Sam. 2:2 and Is. 40:25), and His presence is holy as well. Moses encountered the holiness of God when he approached the burning bush and God spoke to him from within the bush.

> **"Do not come any closer," God said. "Take off your sandals, for the place where you are standing is holy ground"** (Exodus 3:5).

Years later Joshua had a similar experience.

> **Now when Joshua was near Jericho, he looked up and saw a Man standing in front of him with a drawn sword in His hand. Joshua went up to Him and asked, "Are You for us or for our enemies?" "Neither," He replied,**

"but as Commander of the army of the Lord I have now come." Then Joshua fell facedown to the ground in reverence, and asked Him, "What message does my Lord have for His servant?" The commander of the Lord's army replied, "Take off your sandals, for the place where you are standing is holy." And Joshua did so (Joshua 5:13-15).

It would seem, then, that Adam became a foreign body, a contaminant, a cancer, if you will, to the presence of God at the time of his fall. Having lost the Holy Spirit, Adam no longer reflected the holiness of God that was his birthright when he was created in God's image. Now Adam's sin made him an affront to the holiness of God. God responded by sending him out from the garden of His presence and by placing cherubim at the entrance of the garden to protect His presence from sinful man.

Protectors of God's Presence

Cherubim are winged angels that are guardians of the Lord's presence. This role is seen not only in the cherubim's station at the entrance to Eden, but also in their presence near the throne of God.

Hear us, O Shepherd of Israel, You who lead Joseph like a flock; You who sit enthroned between the cherubim, shine forth (Psalm 80:1).

The Lord reigns, let the nations tremble; He sits enthroned between the cherubim, let the earth shake (Psalm 99:1).

O Lord Almighty, God of Israel, enthroned between the cherubim, You alone are God over all the kingdoms of the earth. You have made heaven and earth (Isaiah 37:16).

This position of protecting the presence of the Lord was particularly evident in the design of the Ark of the Covenant, where the cherubim, with outspread wings, guarded the Mercy Seat where God dwelt on top of the Ark. So when the priests went in to the Most Holy Place, the cherubim were the first beings the priests saw. Before they could get to God, they had to get past the cherubim. Anything or anyone contaminated by sin that approached God's presence would never get past the cherubim because sinful things and people could not enter God's presence lest they be consumed by Him.[2]

The prophet Ezekiel describes the cherubim as having four wings and four faces, and they were covered with eyes:

> **And within it there were figures resembling four living beings. And this was their appearance: they had human form. Each of them had four faces and four wings. And their legs were straight and their feet were like a calf's hoof, and they gleamed like burnished bronze. Under their wings on their four sides were human hands. As for the faces and wings of the four of them, their wings touched one another; their faces did not turn when they moved, each went straight forward. As for the form of their faces, each had the face of a man, all four had the face of a lion on the right and the face of a bull on the left, and all four had the face of an eagle. Such were their faces. Their wings were spread out above; each had two touching another being, and two covering their bodies** (Ezekiel 1:5-11 NAS).

> **Their entire bodies, including their backs, their hands and their wings, were completely full of eyes....Each of**

---

2. The inability of our holy God to tolerate sin in His presence is what caused Jesus to cry out while on the cross, "My God, My God, why have You forsaken Me?" (Mt. 27:46) The eternal fellowship between the Father and the Son was broken in those moments as Jesus hung on the cross, bearing the sin of the world.

the cherubim had four faces: One face was that of a cherub, the second the face of a man, the third the face of a lion, and the fourth the face of an eagle (Ezekiel 10:12-14).

The task of guarding the presence of God is also evidently shared by another group of winged angels called seraphim. Isaiah saw these angels when he received his call to be a prophet:

In the year that King Uzziah died, I saw the Lord seated on a throne, high and exalted, and the train of His robe filled the temple. Above Him were seraphs, each with six wings: With two wings they covered their faces, with two they covered their feet, and with two they were flying. And they were calling to one another: "Holy, holy, holy is the Lord Almighty; the whole earth is full of His glory." At the sound of their voices the doorposts and thresholds shook and the temple was filled with smoke. "Woe to me!" I cried. "I am ruined! For I am a man of unclean lips, and I live among a people of unclean lips, and my eyes have seen the King, the Lord Almighty." Then one of the seraphs flew to me with a live coal in his hand, which he had taken with tongs from the altar. With it he touched my mouth and said, "See, this has touched your lips; your guilt is taken away and your sin atoned for" (Isaiah 6:1-7).

We see here that the seraphim not only protected the holiness of God; they also met Isaiah's need when he recognized his sinfulness in the presence of a holy God. Thus, their role was both to protect God's presence and to preserve man when he recognized his sinfulness and repented.

Please note that these angels, or living creatures or beings, as they are often called, didn't protect man from God; they protected God's presence from man. Their task was to prevent man from getting into God's presence—his intended environment and therefore the place where he functions properly, despite his sin and his loss of holiness. For you see, man despite his sin is still made in the image of God. His sinful behavior has not changed his basic make-up. What has changed is man's ability to act like God acts.

This is true because man lost the Holy Spirit when he sinned and therefore no longer has the capacity to function from the spiritual and moral character of God. In other words, man is still spirit just like God is Spirit, but he is no longer truth and righteousness, as God is (see Ps. 31:5; 45:4). This is why David, after his sin with Bathsheba, sought God with these words,

> **Create in me a pure heart, O God, and renew a steadfast spirit within me. Do not cast me from Your presence or take Your Holy Spirit from me** (Psalm 51:10-11).

David knew that his heart and spirit were not right with God because of his sin, and that God had every right to withdraw His presence from David's life.

Sinners Are Malfunctioning Saints

This condition of a heart and spirit that are not right with God has been man's plight ever since the first man and woman chose disobedience over obedience. Adam and Eve certainly appeared to be functioning fine after they left the garden in that they lived to be more than 900 years old. In truth, they were *mal*functioning fine. Adam was still working the ground and having kids as God had intended when He first created man. Nevertheless, Adam was completely malfunctioning because nothing outside its intended environment can function properly. Adam couldn't function like he'd been designed to do because the absence of God's presence made it impossible for him to live like God had planned he would live.

This is why Adam is said to have died when he sinned. Although his physical being didn't die immediately, Adam did die spiritually in the exact moment he was cut off from God's presence because death is the absence of the presence of God in a man or a woman's life. So we see that the man God had pronounced to be "very good" (see Gen. 1:31) became very wrong because he had lost his ideal environment. He was a good creation in the wrong place and thus began to malfunction (sin).

This is the whole problem with our world today. Men and women are malfunctioning (sinning) because they cannot function properly apart from God. This condition of malfunction would have continued indefinitely had God not intervened to rescue the human beings that He had created with His image and likeness. While we were yet unable to return to His presence because we were contaminated by sin, God died for us.

Death is the absence of God's presence in your life.

> You see, at just the right time, when we were still powerless, Christ died for the ungodly. Very rarely will anyone die for a righteous man, though for a good man someone might possibly dare to die. But God demonstrates His own love for us in this: While we were still sinners, Christ died for us. Since we have now been justified by His blood, how much more shall we be saved from God's wrath through Him! For if, when we were God's enemies, we were reconciled to Him through the death of His Son, how much more, having been reconciled, shall we be saved through His life! (Romans 5:6-10)

God came to our rescue because He wants His family back. He knows that sin is the malfunctioning of a saint, and that saints who are in the wrong environment are incapable of functioning correctly, so He sought to restore us to our right environment.

Since God's work of restoration is a work in process, the evidence of man's estrangement from God because of his lost holiness is a constant refrain throughout the history of God's dealings with His people. Indeed, no generation escaped this slavery to sin as "again and again they put God to the test [and] vexed the Holy One of Israel" (Ps. 78:41) until God dealt with them because of their sin. Moses and Aaron, who lost the opportunity to lead God's people into the Promised Land because they neglected to honor the Lord's holiness before the people, are but an example of the many who have suffered because of their unwillingness—and indeed their inability because of their separation from God—to be holy as God is holy.

> **But the Lord said to Moses and Aaron, "Because you did not trust in Me enough to honor Me as holy in the sight of the Israelites, you will not bring this community into the land I give them." These were the waters of Meribah, where the Israelites quarreled with the Lord and where He showed Himself holy among them** (Numbers 20:12-13).

Before the fall it was easy for man to get to God—God's presence was where he spent every moment of every day—and to be holy as God is holy—that was man's innate nature. Once man sinned, however, things changed because he lost the right to be with God every day.

Now God has to deal with all our sin, iniquity, and rebellion before He can let us get near His holy place. And even when we get there, we will find cherubim and seraphim hovering around God to prevent us from approaching Him before our sin is atoned for.

Restoring you to your garden home has been God's plan all along. You are valuable to God despite your sin. Your only problem is that you are in a bad environment, an environment that is something other than where God created you to live. So Jesus paid the exact price you are worth. He laid down His image to buy you back because He knows that although you are a sinner, you still retain His image. In other words, your value didn't change when your environment changed, so God devised a plan to redeem you and to restore you to His presence.

Truly every act of God since man's fall from His presence has been done to restore the relationship that man severed through sin. The entire Old Testament, from Genesis to Malachi, is the story of God's efforts to put man back into the garden environment that he lost.

Please note that the Bible is the story of *God's* efforts, not man's, to restore things to the way they once were. Man cannot accomplish this task alone. He cannot regain his proper environment without the help of his Creator. Truly he cannot even know what is his proper environment and how he was made to function unless God provides the way to bring him back. Man cannot overcome his sin apart from his Savior.

> **God wants His family back.**

Man's inability to restore the communion with God that was broken by sin has not stopped him from trying to reestablish this connection. The many religions of the world and the increased interest in spiritual things in our generation show just how hard man has tried and still is trying to become reconnected with God. Man, when he is living apart from the presence of God, knows that he is lost and empty, with no anchor or foundation for his soul. Whether or not he understands the reason for this void in his life, he feels the effects of it and often spends much time, effort, and money trying to fix his problem.

Nevertheless, none of our self-help books, spiritual exercises, or occult rituals can fulfill our spiritual need. God's prescription for our sin is the only one that works. The only way we become reconnected with God is to accept His gift of salvation through Jesus Christ to cleanse us from all sin. The only way we can stay connected is to practice His presence on a daily basis. Sadly, our refusal to accept God's prescription for sin is quite evident in our sin-filled world.

Do you know why you keep sinning? You sin because you stop, or have never started, practicing the presence of God. It's tough to sin and fellowship with God at the same time. This truth is why you must practice the presence of the Lord all day long.

"How do I practice the presence of God?" you may ask. "Through praise and worship" is the answer. When you are at your job, just hum a song. It's hard to cuss, to gossip, or to complain when you're humming a song. When someone does something to hurt you or to make things difficult for you, just start praying or singing in tongues. You can't get angry when you are talking to God and singing His praises.

This is quite different from what people used to say when I was growing up, "Look, I can put my religion on the side for a minute." What they meant was, "I'll stop worshiping, I'll stop practicing the presence of God for a minute so I can curse you. Then I'll pick it back up again when I've finished taking care of you." God doesn't intend that we live like this. He designed us to always be with Him. He planned that we would never have to function without Him. He wanted us to know the joy, peace, and power of living with Him: "In Thy presence is fulness of joy; at Thy right hand there are pleasures for evermore" (Ps. 16:11b KJV). Joy and pleasures are God's gifts for His children when they stay in the environment He planned for them. So if you stay in God's presence, you will always please Him. Then you won't have to fight anybody because He'll do it for you. Indeed, He will make your enemies your footstool (see Ps. 110:1).

> **T**he Bible is our Manufacturer's program to put us, His product, back into our ideal environment.

Praise and worship are God's solutions to get us back into His presence. We must be clear, however, that praise and worship don't put us back into God's presence; they bring God's presence *to* us. That is, they are but the means that provide the conditions that invite God to come to us as He came to Adam and Eve in the cool of the day. They are the tools that set the stage for God's arrival.

All salvation history is the story of God's efforts to do just this: to reestablish the conditions where He can live with His people as He did in the garden. He is our Source and our Manufacturer. Therefore, He is the only One who knows both what He created us to do (our purpose) and where He designed us to succeed (our ideal environment). He is also the only One who can help us regain all that we lost through sin.

❖ PRINCIPLES ❖

1. Everything in life was created to function within a specific environment.

2. Man's ideal environment is the presence of God.

3. Man's sin has separated him from his ideal environment.

4. Sinners are malfunctioning saints. Therefore, all our problems stem from the fact that we have lost our ideal environment.

5. God is holy. He cannot allow sin to enter His presence.

6. Salvation through Jesus Christ is the only means by which we can return to God's presence.

7. Praise and worship are God's gifts to restore His presence to man.

Chapter 3

Creating a Dwelling Place for God

**God's goal throughout history has been
to get man back into His presence.**

God is in the restoration business, and the Bible is a record of His efforts to get us back into His presence. Therefore, the stories in the Old Testament are not primarily about the patriarchs, judges, kings, and prophets, or about the victories and defeats of God's people. Rather, the Bible can be summed up as an account of God's acts to get man back into His ideal environment. It tells of God's basic desire: "I want a place on earth where I can put My presence again because I need to rescue this malfunctioning machine called 'man.' "

This work of God to get man back into His ideal environment reached its climax in the life, death, and resurrection of Jesus, God's Son. Everything Jesus did was to get God's presence back into man's experience. This is why He had to shed His blood.

God's temple, namely us, had become unholy, so God had to cleanse us and make us holy again through the sacrificial death and the poured-out blood of His Son. Truly, we cannot be qualified to receive the presence of God into our life until the blood of Jesus cleanses us and makes way for the return of God's Spirit to our human temples. Therefore, the key to the continuing work of Jesus in each of us is the Holy Spirit. When the Spirit is alive and well in us, He restores the presence of God to our life and leads us into the holiness that was our birthright at creation.

However, long before God sent Jesus and the Holy Spirit, man attempted to bridge the gap that his sin had created between him and God. These early attempts at worship begin in the Book of Genesis.

Altars for God

Man's first act of worship is recorded in Genesis chapter 4, right after the story in Genesis 3 of man's sin and his fall from God's presence.

In the course of time Cain brought some of the fruits of the soil as an offering to the Lord. But Abel brought fat portions from some of the firstborn of his flock (Genesis 4:3-4a).

What were Cain and Abel doing here? They were trying to get back into touch with God. They evidently knew they needed to be in communication with God. This effort to get God's presence back into man's life is evident throughout the Old Testament. Repeatedly, God's people built altars to prepare a place for the presence of God to come and offered sacrifices either to invite God to come or to commemorate a time and a place where He had come.

Altars prepare a place for the presence of God to come.

After the offerings given by Cain and Abel, the next record in the Bible of man's attempt to communicate with God through sacrifices and offerings is found in the story of Noah. After the flood, when Noah, his family, and all the animals had emerged from the ark, Noah built an altar and offered burnt offerings unto God.

The Lord smelled the pleasing aroma and said in His heart: "Never again will I curse the ground because of man, even though every inclination of his heart is evil from childhood. And never again will I destroy all living creatures, as I have done. As long as the earth endures, seedtime and harvest, cold and heat, summer and winter, day and night will never cease." Then God blessed Noah and his sons, saying to them, "Be fruitful and increase in number and fill the earth" (Genesis 8:21–9:1).

Please notice that God is pleased with Noah's attempts to communicate with Him. Hence, God blesses Noah and his sons. Nonetheless, Noah is still a malfunctioning man. This is, perhaps, most evident in the blessing that God gives to Noah, "Be fruitful and increase in number and fill the earth." This blessing is very similar to God's blessing of the first man and the first woman (see Gen. 1:28), but an important element is missing. God does not command Noah to subdue the earth and to rule over the fish of the sea, the birds of the air, and over every living creature. Why? Through his sin, man has lost both his right and his power to dominate the earth. He gave that right to satan, whom Jesus refers to as the "prince of this world" (see Jn. 14:30). Therefore, although man is again communicating with God, this relationship does not have the moment-by-moment intimacy of the garden fellowship that God and man had enjoyed.

Friends With God

Abraham

Abraham (Abram) is the next man whom the Scriptures tell us built an altar to the Lord. This follows God's appearance to him when God promised Abraham that He would give the land of Canaan to Abraham's offspring (see Gen. 12:7). This is but the first of many altars that Abraham built to God. Perhaps the most well-known altar Abraham built was the one on Mount Moriah when God commanded him to offer his son Isaac as a burnt offering (see Gen. 22). This story shows why Abraham was regarded by God as His friend. Not only was Abraham a worshiper (as is evidenced by the number of altars he built), but so great was Abraham's commitment to, passion for, and trust in God that he gave Him even his son, the son of promise. Believing that God would provide a lamb for the sacrifice, yet not knowing that at the very last minute God would provide a ram to take the son's place, Abraham bound Isaac on the altar and raised his hand to kill him. Only God's voice stopped him from giving God what He had asked for.

David

As is often true in the Bible, the place of one sacrifice becomes the place of another. This time the worshiper is David. He has sinned by counting the fighting men of Israel and God has shown His displeasure by sending a plague on the people. When David sees the carnage among his people, he entreats God to punish him, not them, because he is the one who has sinned. God, through the prophet Gad, then tells David to build an altar on the threshing floor of Araunah (later associated with Mt. Moriah where Abraham offered up Isaac; see 2 Chron. 3:1) so that the plague may stop.

This was certainly not the only time David built an altar to the Lord. As a youth tending his father's sheep, he had learned to seek the presence of Yahweh. These early experiences with God influenced him so much that when faced with the choice of three years of famine, three months of fleeing from his enemies, or three days of plague, David chose the plague.

I am in deep distress. Let us fall into the hands of the Lord, for His mercy is great; but do not let me fall into the hands of men (2 Samuel 24:14b).

Do you see why David chose the third option? He preferred to fall into the hands of God rather than the hands of men. Why would David choose God over man? David knew the God he had sung to as a shepherd boy playing his harp. Now, when he is king and is faced with a difficult decision that means suffering not only for him but for his people, David draws on what he had learned during those years of private worship before he entered the public eye. He knows that God is good and His mercy endures forever, so he entrusts himself and his kingdom to God.

David's lasting relationship with God is also seen when he takes Bathsheba, another man's wife, to his bed and tries to cover his sin. When the prophet Nathan confronts him, David immediately responds, "I have sinned against the Lord" (2 Sam. 12:13b). He doesn't argue or make excuses. He accepts the truth of Nathan's words and the justice of God's punishment.

> *P*raise must be learned in private before it is exhibited in public.

The Lord has taken away your sin. You are not going to die. But because by doing this you have made the enemies of the Lord show utter contempt, the son born to you will die (2 Samuel 12:13b-14).

Psalm 51, written during this time in David's life, shows just how much he valued the presence of the Lord. Although he interceded for his son's life while the child still lived, David didn't criticize God for taking him. In truth, Psalm 51 shows that David thought of a punishment far worse than the loss of his son:

Create in me a pure heart, O God, and renew a steadfast spirit within me. Do not cast me from Your presence or

take Your Holy Spirit from me. Restore to me the joy of Your salvation and grant me a willing spirit, to sustain me (Psalm 51:10-12).

You see, David was used to having his own private worship services. He knew the joy and power of living with God. He also knew what happens to a man when sin takes the presence of God from his life.

As a young man, David had played his harp for King Saul when an evil spirit tormented him. This spirit came to Saul after the Lord had departed from his life because of his failure to obey God. The memories of those hours with Saul surely contributed to David's own plea that God not take His Spirit from him. He knew the misery man endures when faced with the absence of God. Losing the Holy Spirit and the presence of God would therefore have been a punishment far greater than the death of his son.

Moses

Moses was another "friend of God." As the leader of a grumbling, dissatisfied people, he often cried out to God. So when God told Moses to take the people up to the Promised Land, but that He would not go with them lest He destroy the people as they traveled, Moses said, "No way!" He wasn't going anywhere unless God was going with him.

Moses said to the Lord, "You have been telling me, 'Lead these people,' but You have not let me know whom You will send with me. You have said, 'I know you by name and you have found favor with Me.' If You are pleased with me, teach me Your ways so I may know You and continue to find favor with You. Remember that this nation is Your people." The Lord replied, "My Presence will go with you, and I will give you rest." Then Moses said to Him, "If Your Presence does not go with us, do not send us up from here" (Exodus 33:12-15).

What was God's response? God agreed to do the very thing Moses asked because He knew Moses by name and was pleased with him.

Like Abraham before him and David after him, Moses was hungry for God. He wanted to know God and to find favor with Him. Not only that, he wanted to see God. It wasn't enough that God spoke to him from the pillar of cloud whenever he entered the Tabernacle and that his face shown with God's glory even after he had left the Tabernacle. Moses wanted to see God face to face.

God knew that Moses' request was a problem. No man in his sinful nature could see God and live. But since Moses was so intent on seeing Him, and because Moses was His friend, God agreed to let Moses see His glory.

What Moses saw... Wow! That must have been some close walk God took past him. What else could Moses do but bow to the ground and worship. He had seen the glory of the Almighty! Now he was more sure than ever that he didn't want to go anywhere if God was not going along. (See Exodus chapter 33.)

Temples for God

The outdoor altars of Cain and Abel, of Noah, of Abraham and his descendants, and of Moses eventually gave way to the enclosed sanctuaries of the Tabernacle and the Temple, but their purpose remained the same. All were places of God's presence, and sacrifices were offered there with the belief that God would accept them and be pleased with them.

In the Tabernacle and the Temple, however, the worship of God became more regulated. Indeed, the building of the Tent and the Temple, as well as the praise and worship offered there, were governed by the specifications of God Himself, with no room for variance.

The Lord said to Moses, "Tell the Israelites to bring Me an offering. You are to receive the offering for Me from

each man whose heart prompts him to give. These are the offerings you are to receive from them: gold, silver and bronze....Then have them make a sanctuary for Me, and I will dwell among them" (Exodus 25:1-3,8).

Do you see what verse 8 says? God wanted a place to live among His people so He told Moses to bring an offering. All this money was not about having a nice building with soft comfortable chairs. God told Moses to gather an offering from the people because He wanted to get His presence in their midst. It wasn't enough for Him to meet with Moses on the mountain. He wanted to live with all His people.

Building a place for God is always about having the presence of God in the midst of His people. In fact, a big fancy building may look like a church and may even be called a church, but in reality it is very far from being one. Why is this? Nothing is happening there.

Building a church for God is not about the building or the equipment. It's about God's presence. If God's presence is not with you, it doesn't matter how elaborate your building is, how well educated your staff are, how well planned your worship services are, or how dynamic the preaching is. Without God's presence all you have is a big building filled with people. On the other hand, you can meet in a plain room with simple worship and an untrained preacher but have everything. The difference is in the absence or the presence of God.

God's presence is the only essential ingredient in worship. Our praise and the other elements of our meetings must lead us into the presence of God. If they don't, there is no reason to do them. Oh, yes, they may be nice and may make us feel good, but the purpose of gathering is to enter the presence of the Lord. Anything that does not contribute to this is simply unnecessary clutter. God's presence in our presence is the only worthwhile end to our meetings.

This was God's entire purpose for instructing Moses to build the Tabernacle: He wanted to get close to His people. Everything God told Moses to do in some way revealed the lost condition of man and unveiled God's plan to rescue man from his wrong environment by getting His presence back in man's presence.

God's blueprint for the meeting place between Himself and man ensured that man could not just stumble or wander into His presence, lest he be consumed by God because of his sin. This is why God's dwelling place was in the central part of the Tabernacle. God was safeguarding His presence to keep it holy. He also gave Moses very specific instructions concerning the priests, the sacrifices and offerings, and the atonement procedures so that nothing profane would come close to Him. Each of the furnishings, bowls, plates, and other utensils were also made according to God's exact instructions, as well as the Tabernacle itself and the curtains that hung within it. Particular attention was given to the Ark of the Covenant, where God would dwell between the cherubim, and to the rest of the inner chamber that was known as the Holy of Holies.

> **God's presence is the only essential ingredient in worship.**

The furnishings in the Tabernacle each revealed something about God's intent concerning His people and His presence among them. In the Outer Court stood the altar of burnt offerings, where the sacrifices of the people were presented to God to atone for their sins. Beyond the altar, closer to the door leading into the Tabernacle, stood the laver, where the rites of purification were done. These washings were probably intended to make the priests and the sacrifices holy. Within the tabernacle in the Inner Court, also called the Holy Place, stood the table of shewbread, on which the priest put the fresh bread of the presence every Sabbath. This was eaten only by priests and only in the Holy Place. Frankincense was also placed on the table of shewbread. This was burnt on the altar of incense, which stood before the veil leading into the Holy of Holies, to make atonement. Across from the table of shewbread stood the golden lampstand or candlestick.

The final part of the tabernacle was the Holy of Holies where the Ark of the Covenant was kept. On the Mercy Seat above the Ark and between the cherubim that were part of the lid to the Ark was the place where God would dwell. Cherubim, the protectors of God's presence, were also woven into the veil that hung between the Inner Court and the Holy of Holies. (See Exodus chapter 25 and following.) All this was part of God's plans and preparations to provide a place where He could live in the midst of His people. The same was true for the Temple in Jerusalem, when God gave the plans to David and entrusted David's son Solomon with the task of building it.

With the coming of Christ, each of the furnishings in the Tabernacle was revealed to be a type of Him. The Tabernacle, the very house of God, was a type of the Church, where God wants to live. The table of shewbread represented the physical body of Christ and the Christ that would be incarnated in the man. The lampstand, which never went out, represented the Word of God and the Holy Spirit. The altar of burnt offerings was a type of the sacrifices of praise that continually arise from God's people. The courtyard, or Outer Court, spoke of the assembling of God's people. Even the material of the priests' clothes and the things in the Ark of the Covenant revealed part of God's plan that would be consummated in Christ. The priests' clothes were linen, not wool, so the priests would not sweat in God's presence. (Sweat represented work. See Exodus chapters 28–29 and Ezekiel 44:17-18.) The articles in the Ark of the Covenant were the tablets of the Ten Commandments, the rod of Aaron that budded, and a little jar of manna that was a reminder of the wilderness. All these represented important things to God. The rod of Aaron represented the death we experience because of sin and the rebirth and new life that come through Christ. It also represented the burial of Jesus Christ and His resurrection. The manna represented God's grace, received through no work of man, and the tablets containing the

Ten Commandments spoke of our helplessness to keep the law of God and thereby be righteous before Him.

When the priests poured the blood on the top of the Ark, it covered all those things that revealed our sin and our lack of grace. Instead of seeing our sin, God and the cherubim who protected His presence saw the blood. Thus, God could come to dwell above the mercy seat without destroying the priest because of his sin and the sin of the people. The law that condemned us was covered by the blood of grace.

Through Jesus, we gain access to every part of God's dwelling place. He is the sacrifice, the blood, the dwelling place, and the presence of God. He is also the One whose death destroyed the veil that separated God's dwelling place from His people. Now everyone has access to God—everyone, that is, who accepts the gift of grace that is made available to us through the life, death, and resurrection of Jesus.

This way provided by God is the same today as it was two thousand years ago. There is no improved savior and no improved blood. The Savior has been, is, and always will be Jesus Christ, and His blood is the only sacrifice sufficient and acceptable to atone for our sins.

Jesus is still the only way to God. There is no improved savior, no improved blood.

We human beings may be looking for new and improved ways to worship, but God is not. He does not want experts in worship. What God wants is people who will follow His instructions every time they approach Him.

This is just the way God is. He isn't looking for change, since He doesn't change. He is the same yesterday, today, and forever (see Heb. 13:8). His bottom line continues to be His passion for getting His presence back into man's experience. This is His plan for the entire human race because Adam carried in him all the nations of the world. Therefore, when God removed Adam from His presence, He removed all the nations as well. Likewise, when Jesus came to earth, He came to restore the Holy Spirit to all mankind. Before He could do this, however, He had to clean us up so that we could receive God's Spirit. He had to cleanse our impurity.

To say that we are impure does not mean that we are dirty, as in the filth of dirt. What it does mean is that we are impure in God's sight. What we believe, what we say, and what we do don't match. This is what impurity is to God. Therefore, God sent Christ to restore a pure heart to us so that we can be integrated in thought, word, and action. Only when our heart is once more pure can we become the temple in which the Holy Spirit lives (see 1 Cor. 3:16; 6:19).

Since the Holy Spirit is God, He is the key to getting us into God's presence today. He is also the only One who can teach us what God requires of us now (see Jn. 14:26). Sadly, many Christians miss the joy of living with the Lord because their hopes are fixed on Heaven and what they will someday gain there. This may be the theology of the hymnbook, but it is not the theology of the Bible. God's purpose is not that we will fly away to Him someday, but that we will live in His presence today in this world. Therefore, all His work through the Old Testament and into the days of Jesus and the Church has been to get us back into the environment where He first put us here on earth. That environment is His presence.

In essence, the issue is not where you are located, but who is located where you are. You need God's presence to function. So wherever He is, be that in Heaven or on earth, you can function there. This makes seeking God and living in His presence today in this life quite important.

Why else would God create a new Heaven and a new earth?

Then I saw a new heaven and a new earth, for the first heaven and the first earth had passed away, and there was no longer any sea (Revelation 21:1).

He's making another environment for us that is like the atmosphere man once enjoyed in the Garden of Eden. This atmosphere will be on earth because we were created to dominate the earth, not Heaven.

Therefore, Heaven is not the fulfillment of your future. Your eternal home will be a new earth.

> **Then I saw a new heaven and a new earth, for the first heaven and the first earth had passed away, and there was no longer any sea. I saw the Holy City, the new Jerusalem, coming down out of heaven from God, prepared as a bride beautifully dressed for her husband....I did not see a temple in the city, because the Lord God Almighty and the Lamb are its temple. The city does not need the sun or the moon to shine on it, for the glory of God gives it light, and the Lamb is its lamp** (Revelation 21:1-2,22-23).

This new earth won't need a sea to provide water or the sun and the moon to provide light because God Himself will be our light and our life. Just as Adam and Eve enjoyed continual fellowship with God in the Garden of Eden, we will wake up every morning in God's presence and go through the whole day with Him. No matter where we are, we will breathe in life.

However, you don't have to wait for this new earth to live with God. He wants to come to you right now. He wants to live in your home today. He can if you will start praising Him and filling your home with testimonies of how great He is and how good He has been to you. Just start bragging about God from a pure heart, and He will come to you right where you are. He'll set up His throne in your house. That's His plan, and He's bringing it to pass in our generation. He's creating a new order where the power of satan is

> *P*raise is the way you get into God's presence.

defeated in your life and in mine simply because we make room for His presence. We know that He wants us to have His presence. The only question is whether we will make room for Him to come to us.

You do this by filling your environment with praise until He comes and fills the place you have made. That's all. There's no more sweating, no more hard work, no more contriving to do this or that to get to God. You make room for Him, and He comes. That's it. And you do this through praise.

❖ PRINCIPLES ❖

1. All God's work throughout history has been to get His presence back into man's environment.

2. Altars, sacrifices, and offerings invite God's presence to come or they commemorate where He has been.

3. God's friends are worshipers.

4. The whole purpose of the Tabernacle and the Temple was to provide a place for God to live in the midst of His people.

5. God's presence is the only essential ingredient in worship.

6. The design and worship of the Tabernacle looked forward to Jesus and the return of the Holy Spirit.

7. God wants His people to follow His instructions when they come to meet with Him.

8. God wants to live with you today.

Chapter 4

The Blessing of Judah

God makes Himself known through praise.

The blessing of Judah is in his name, which is based on the Hebrew word *yadah*. *Yadah* means "to revere or worship with extended hands," "to make confession," "to praise," or "to give thanks, thankful, thanksgiving" (Strong's, H3034). Thus, Judah's name is literally a word for praise. "Why is this a blessing?" you may ask. Praise is what attracts God's presence to us.

*P*raise is God's prescription for changing your environment.

Leah very well could have chosen another name for her son, a name that would not have brought him nearly so much blessing. After all, she was the unloved wife of Jacob, who preferred her younger sister, Rachel, to her. So wretched was Leah's life that God showed her mercy and allowed her to have children while Rachel was barren.

Even this, however, did not cause Jacob to love her. Yet, after naming her first son, Reuben—because God had seen and responded to her misery—and her second son, Simeon—because she was unloved—Leah chose to praise God in the naming of her third son.

God was evidently pleased with the name that Leah chose for her son. He loved Judah (see Ps. 78:67-68) and chose him to receive special favor. This was not so for Reuben and Simeon, Judah's older brothers, or for any of the other of Jacob's 12 sons. Certainly, God could have chosen any of Jacob's sons to receive the blessing of being the ancestor of King David and of the Messiah, but God chose Judah.

> **The Lord, the God of Israel, chose me [David] from my whole family to be king over Israel forever. He chose Judah as leader, and from the house of Judah He chose my family, and from my father's sons He was pleased to make me king over all Israel** (1 Chronicles 28:4).

The significance of the tribe of Judah as seen in both the Old and New Testaments bears witness to this special favor that God bestowed on Judah. In the Old Testament, Judah and his descendants are recognized leaders, a responsibility foretold by his father, Jacob, when he blessed his sons.

> **Judah, your brothers will praise you; your hand will be on the neck of your enemies; your father's sons will bow down to you. You are a lion's cub, O Judah; you return from the prey, my son. Like a lion he crouches and lies down, like a lioness—who dares to rouse him? The scepter will not depart from Judah, nor the ruler's staff from between his feet, until he comes to whom it belongs and the obedience of the nations is his. He will tether his donkey to a vine, his colt to the choicest branch; he will wash his garments in wine, his robes in the blood of grapes. His eyes will be darker than wine, his teeth whiter than milk** (Genesis 49:8-12).

The leadership of Judah is also seen in other Old Testament passages. In the Book of Judges, when the tribes of Israel go to war against the tribe of Benjamin, God tells the Israelites that Judah should be the tribe to lead them into battle:

The Israelites went up to Bethel and inquired of God. They said, "Who of us shall go first to fight against the Benjamites?" The Lord replied, "Judah shall go first" (Judges 20:18).

At the dedication of the wall around Jerusalem after the exile, the leaders of Judah were stationed on the walls with two choirs (see Neh. 12:27-31). In addition, in the Psalms, Judah is described as God's scepter:

Gilead is Mine, Manasseh is Mine; Ephraim is My helmet, Judah My scepter (Psalm 108:8).

A scepter is the instrument that a king holds in his hand to represent his authority and power. To say that Judah is God's scepter, is thus to say that he is a representative of God's authority and power. This is first fulfilled in King David and his descendants, and ultimately in Jesus Christ, the Messiah. In the New Testament, God's authority revealed in and through the tribe of Judah is seen in Revelation 5:5, where Jesus is called the Lion from the tribe of Judah. Judah is also listed in Revelation 7:5 at the head of the tribes who are to be sealed at the end of time.

The favor of God in Judah's life is also seen in Psalm 114:2, where Judah is described as God's sanctuary:

Judah became God's sanctuary, Israel His dominion.

The Hebrew word translated here as *sanctuary* means "a sacred place or thing," "consecrated, dedicated, hallowed, holiness, holy, saint, sanctuary" (Strong's, H6944). In other words, God's government and His ruling power were evident in the whole of Israel, but Judah was His headquarters, the distinctive place of His dwelling.

As such, Judah experienced God's presence in a way the other tribes did not. Jerusalem and Mount Zion, the mountain on which the Temple stood, were within its boundaries.

> **In Judah God is known; His name is great in Israel. His tent is in Salem, His dwelling place in Zion** (Psalm 76:1-2).

Perhaps this is why the tribe of Judah, the southern kingdom, was spared by God long after He destroyed the northern 11 tribes for their apostasy (see 2 Kings 17:18). God was preserving the place of His presence. Might it also be that the Mercy Seat of God among the people of Judah kept their heart turned toward God longer than the hearts of their brothers in the north who did not have this blessing? In any case, God's favor toward Judah caused Him to set up His headquarters in the midst of this tribe. He made Judah His dwelling place, the place of His presence.

The Message of Judah

If the dwelling place of God is in Judah, what does this say to us about the significance of Judah? What can we learn from this story so we too may receive the blessing and favor of the Lord that Judah enjoyed? To answer this, let's rephrase some of the Scripture quotations from above, inserting the word *praise* wherever the word *Judah* is used.

- The hand of praise will be on the neck of your enemies (see Gen. 49:8).

- Praise shall go first (see Judg. 20:18).

- Praise is God's authority and power (see Ps. 108:8).

- In praise, God is known (see Ps. 76:1).

- Praise is God's dwelling place (see Ps. 76:2; 114:2).

Wow! That's a rather impressive assessment of the purpose and power of praise. Praise is how you come to know God. Praise is God's dwelling place, His sphere of influence and authority in your life. In essence, God will show up if you praise Him in the midst of your darkest moments.

This is what Leah, the mother of Judah, did. She chose to praise God through the naming of her son instead of telling the world how terrible things were for her. She held a private little praise session despite the scorn of her husband and her sister. The result was, God came to her and put His hand of favor on her son.

So often we go looking for God when we could be creating an environment that invites Him to come to us. In fact, our human tendency to look for God is the reason we have so many religions in our world. People are looking for God. They know they need Him but they don't know how to get Him. No matter which of the world's religions you study, you will soon find that they are all motivated by the same thing. Man universally and instinctively knows that he needs God, and all his religious beliefs and activities are his efforts to find Him.

This is why I sympathize with those who worship other gods. They are looking for what I have found. They are looking for God, the Creator of the world. They are looking for Jesus, the Savior of the world. They are looking for the Holy Spirit, God's truth in the world. Most people probably would not define their search and their religious practices in these terms, but man is universally searching for God. We all have this built-in awareness that life as it is does not match life as we need it to be.

> **All human beings experience an emptiness or void when God is absent.**

Therefore, man's religious exercises are simply his means of trying to find the presence of God. That's why I can walk up to a

Buddhist, a Muslim, or a Hindu with great confidence. I know who they are looking for, and He is part of my life.

Sadly, people of other religions are not the only ones who are looking for God. Many Christians are too. Perhaps you are one of them. You spend much time and effort looking for Him when you don't have to look for Him at all. He will come to you if you will just praise Him.

Actually, when you learn to live in praise, folks will automatically see God in you. They will recognize His presence with you and will see His authority at work in your life. Then they'll say to you, "What makes you so happy?" to which you'll have the wisdom to respond, "I'm in my ideal environment, Brother." "I have my own private incubator all around me every day, Sister."

Even when your life is full of problems, as it sometimes will be, others will notice that your response is different from that of other people and they'll ask you, "Why aren't you afraid? How can you be so calm in the midst of such frightening circumstances?" You can then reply, "I'm not afraid because when troubles and problems come my way, I run to the dwelling place of my God through praise and I am safe."

Just imagine the difference a consistent pattern of praise could make in your life. It would be like having a child named Judah. Every time you spoke to him by name, you would be praising God: "Praise God, come here." "Praise God, do your homework." "Praise God, it's time to go to sleep." Day after day your house would be filled with praise: "Praise God, I had an accident but I'm not hurt." "Praise God, I lost my job but we still have enough money to pay the rent." "Praise God, my back hurts, but I can still walk."

> **P**raise is your access, your key, into the presence of God.

Truly, the blessing of Judah was in his name and in the favor God showed to him because of his name. The same can be true for you. You can receive the same blessings Judah and his descendants did—the presence of God, the power and authority of God, the victory of God over the difficulties of your life—through your offerings of praise. These blessings are yours because God dwells in the people who praise Him as He requires.

❖ PRINCIPLES ❖

1. The name *Judah* means "praise."

2. God chose Judah for special blessing.

3. Judah was the dwelling place of God.

4. Praise is the dwelling place of God.

5. All people are seeking God.

6. When we praise God, we don't have to look for Him because He comes to us.

Chapter 5

What Is Praise?

Praise is celebrating God as our heart's true home.

The Scriptures are filled with injunctions to praise the Lord:

Then David said to the whole assembly, "Praise the Lord your God." So they all praised the Lord, the God of their fathers; they bowed low and fell prostrate before the Lord and the king (1 Chronicles 29:20).

Praise the Lord. Give thanks to the Lord, for He is good; His love endures forever (Psalm 106:1).

Praise the Lord. Praise, O servants of the Lord, praise the name of the Lord (Psalm 113:1).

Praise the Lord, all you nations; extol Him, all you peoples (Psalm 117:1).

Let everything that has breath praise the Lord. Praise the Lord (Psalm 150:6).

If we are to obey these commands from God, we must first learn what praise is. *Praise* includes commending; expressing approval or a favorable judgment of; and glorifying, especially by crediting with perfections (see Webster's, "praise").

Definitions of Praise

Commending

To *commend* someone is "to entrust for care or preservation" or "to recommend as worthy of confidence or notice" (Webster's, "commend"). Praising God by commendation thus means that we entrust ourselves to His care and recommend that others do the same. The Psalms of David, in particular, are filled with testimonies of the Lord's trustworthiness, and with expressions of confidence that He will again prove Himself trustworthy.

O Lord my God, in Thee do I put my trust: save me from all them that persecute me, and deliver me (Psalm 7:1 KJV).

Those who know Your name will trust in You, for You, Lord, have never forsaken those who seek You (Psalm 9:10).

Preserve me, O God: for in Thee do I put my trust (Psalm 16:1 KJV).

Some trust in chariots and some in horses, but we trust in the name of the Lord our God (Psalm 20:7).

Praise by commendation thus applies the promises of God to our personal circumstances. Let's say, for example, that a father has just lost his job and he's concerned how he will provide for his family. Perhaps his heart is heavy and he's feeling overwhelmed by the future. His praise of God in such a situation might go something like this:

> *Lord God, You are my provider. I praise You, for I know that You care for me and You care for my family. You are the God who cares even for the sparrows, and I know that my wife, my children, and I are worth much more to You than the sparrows are. Therefore, I choose not to worry. Instead I will boast of Your goodness to us in the past, for there have been other times, Father God, when we didn't know how we were going to pay our bills. Yet, You have always made a way, even when there seemed to be no way. Thank You for Your goodness. Thank You for Your care and provision. I know that I can trust You. I know that Your eyes are on my family and You will not forget us. Even as You provided food for Your people as they wandered through the wilderness, today I declare by faith that You will provide for us too. You alone are my refuge. I choose not to be shaken by fear. You alone are the source of all I have and ever hope to have. I praise You because You are faithful. You are the Everlasting One. I know that You are aware of what we are going through, and I thank You in advance for what You will do for us. To Your name be the glory today, tomorrow, next week, and next month in my life. I praise You and honor You. You are my God.*

Expressing Approval or Favorable Judgment

To *approve* of someone is "to have or express a favorable opinion" of him or to show esteem (Webster's, "approve"). Personal experience is at the heart of this expression of praise as well. Here again, the Psalms contain numerous examples of personal expressions of approval toward God.

But You, O God, do see trouble and grief; You consider it to take it in hand. The victim commits himself to You; You are the helper of the fatherless (Psalm 10:14).

But I will sing of Your strength, in the morning I will sing of Your love; for You are my fortress, my refuge in times of trouble (Psalm 59:16).

O God, You are my God, earnestly I seek You; my soul thirsts for You, my body longs for You, in a dry and weary land where there is no water. I have seen You in the sanctuary and beheld Your power and Your glory (Psalm 63:1-2).

So you see, praise by approving is turning our thoughts toward God and remembering how He has won our acclaim. It's reciting the wonder of who He is and how He has made a difference in our life and the life of others. Many Scriptures do this, but Psalm 23 is perhaps the most well-known passage of Scripture that is a personal recommendation for God. David praises God by describing Him as the Shepherd who cares for David, His sheep. Each image from the life and work of a shepherd in some way speaks to David of God's work in his own life.

This is why Psalm 23 is such a wonderful Scripture portion to use during private praise and worship. It encourages you, the worshiper, to see and celebrate God's personal care shown in your life and to express your adoration and gratitude to God for His goodness to you. To do this, you might read or recite a line from the Psalm, then praise God for how it's been true in your life. As you praise Him, you will find that you are building an impressive resumé of God's greatness, faithfulness, and love as you've experienced Him.

The Lord is my Shepherd.... My God, You are an awesome God. Even before I was born, You had a plan for my life. You are the Alpha and Omega who sees my tomorrows when I can't face today. You are the Faithful One who seeks Your sheep even when I wander from the paths You have chosen for me. You are the Tender One who comforts me when I am sad or lonely and heals me when I am hurt. You are the Forgiving One who looks beyond my failures to what I yet can be. You are the Loving and Merciful One who loves me even when I am unlovely and does good to me despite the fact that I don't deserve it....

I shall not want...*because You are always meeting my needs. You have given me a good mind so I can learn things quickly. You have given me a job I like and an employer who is understanding and fair. You have blessed me and my family with a warm, dry house and an abundance of food in our refrigerator and our cupboards. We have never gone hungry or lacked clothes to wear because You have provided for our needs. Thank You for being so good to us. Thank You for providing even more than we need....*

Many Scriptures that don't use the words associated with praise—words like *thank*, *sing*, *honor*, or *worship*—can be used in this manner. Why is this? They record glimpses of someone's favorable opinion of God, glimpses that invite us to praise Him as well by expressing our approval of Him and our gratitude for His grace and mercy shown to us throughout our life. In essence, praise that approves is like writing a letter of recommendation for God!

Glorifying

To *glorify* someone is to "bestow honor, praise, or admiration" (Webster's, "glorify"). In other words, giving glory to someone specifically identifies what is admirable in the person. This type of praise is also quite frequent in the Scriptures. God is recognized as being good (e.g. Ps. 34:8), faithful (e.g. Ps. 33:4), righteous (e.g. Ps. 11:7), just (e.g. 2 Chron. 12:6), and merciful and forgiving (e.g. Dan. 9:9), to name a few. In addition, God, His dwelling place, His law, His character, and His actions are described as being perfect and flawless:

As for God, His way is perfect; the word of the Lord is flawless. He is a shield for all who take refuge in Him (2 Samuel 22:31).

The law of the Lord is perfect, reviving the soul. The statutes of the Lord are trustworthy, making wise the simple (Psalm 19:7).

O Lord, You are my God; I will exalt You and praise Your name, for in perfect faithfulness You have done marvelous things, things planned long ago (Isaiah 25:1).

Be perfect, therefore, as your heavenly Father is perfect (Matthew 5:48).

Every good and perfect gift is from above, coming down from the Father of the heavenly lights, who does not change like shifting shadows (James 1:17).

Psalm 103, in particular, is a good example of Scripture that glorifies God. In this Psalm, David lists some of the many praiseworthy benefits of knowing God. God forgives our sin (vs. 3), heals our diseases (vs. 3), redeems our life (vs. 4), crowns us with love and compassion (vs. 4), satisfies us with good things (vs. 5), works righteousness and justice for the oppressed (vs. 6), is slow to anger (vs. 8), does not always accuse (vs. 9), does not keep His anger forever (vs. 9), does not treat us as our sin deserves (vs. 10), and removes our transgressions from us (vs. 12).

I'm sure you see how one or all of these benefits may be the basis for a praise service, whether private or public. Surely, all of us recall times when God worked in our life in one or more of these ways. Praising God by glorifying Him is simply recognizing and testifying to all these admirable qualities of God. For example, it's saying, "Yes, I know God works for the oppressed. My boss was always belittling me in front of the rest of the crew and laughing at me when I didn't work as fast as he thought I should. I never said anything, although I was plenty angry inside. I just asked God to give me strength and to be my advocate. Yesterday I found out that my boss is being moved to another plant. God is so good. He's so good to me." It's saying, "God has every reason to write me off forever. Many times He has helped me get clean from drugs, but

I've always gone back—usually to a stronger addiction than He saved me from. Yet, I know He loves me, and He forgives me every time I repent. I thank Him for His goodness to me. I don't deserve it, but that doesn't seem to stop Him from loving me and from reaching out to me when I get myself into a mess again. He has sent so many people to me who have helped me see His love and mercy. He is one awesome God. I don't understand why, but I know He cares for me, and He hears my cries when I plead for His help. Why don't you try Him for yourself? You'll find that He's faithful to you too."

Another way we honor God is to recite His names or other designations of who He is. For example: "The Lord is a warrior" (Ex. 15:3a). "The Lord is God in heaven above and on the earth below. There is no other" (Deut. 4:39b). "...the Lord is [my] life..." (Deut. 30:20). "...the hand of the Lord is powerful..." (Josh. 4:24). "...The Lord is Peace..." (Judg. 6:24). "The Lord is a God who knows, and by Him deeds are weighed" (1 Sam. 2:3b). "The Lord is my rock, my fortress and my deliverer" (2 Sam. 22:2). "The Lord is King" (Ps. 10:16a). "The Lord is my light and my salvation" (Ps. 27:1a). "The Lord is the strength of His people" (Ps. 28:8a).

As we honor God for who He is and for what He has done in our lives, we make room for Him to work for us and in us every day. We give Him a place to dwell in the midst of our life because we refuse to take His benefits to us for granted. We know we are sinners saved by grace, and we give Him the glory for saving us and for being there for us when we need Him.

Characteristics of Praise

Praise Puts God in First Place

Praise is always turning our attention from ourselves to God. It's remembering and recounting who He is and what He has done, instead of wallowing in the mire of self-absorption. Truly, we are incredibly self-centered people. Our first thought is always how something or someone is affecting us.

Praise turns our eyes from ourselves to God. It focuses our thoughts on His majesty and power and invites others to do the same. Instead of gazing at our own navel, we raise our eyes and our heart to see His face and to affirm again our awe of Him, our gratitude for His love and mercy, and our absolute dependence on Him.

In essence, praise is bragging about God instead of us or the idols of this world. It's celebrating who He is and how He relates to His people. Many Christians and congregations rarely do this. We are so self-focused that we treat praise and worship as preliminaries that we have to get through to get to the important stuff, which of course is the teaching and personal ministry that make us feel good. Sadly, we all too often treat our expressions of admiration toward God as though He is of secondary importance.

I'm sure God is not pleased with this behavior. Indeed, there's no reason to have a meeting if praise and worship are not the central focus of our time together. We may call our collection of traditions, habits, and activities "worship," but we have no hope of worshiping God if we are not willing to first give Him the praise that is His due.

Praise Flows From Our Friendship With God

People who praise God on a regular basis do so because they have found the Lord to be so altogether lovely that they can't stop thinking of Him and talking of Him. They have gotten close enough to Him to see His true nature and character, and they have found in Him more than everything they have ever hoped for.

You see, you can't brag about someone you don't know—at least your bragging cannot be truthful and sincere. Therefore, although praise may start with what you know *about* God, it must eventually progress to what you yourself have experienced of Him.

This is when praise becomes more than a chore or a duty. You don't have to work up your praise because it automatically bubbles up from within you. Your relationship with God has confirmed for you that you are blessed at all times. He is your joy, your strength, your comfort, your peace, and on and on. Your life is anchored in Him, and His goodness to you brings His name to your thoughts and your lips repeatedly.

In other words, praise that flows from a deep relationship with God is genuine and true. Your words and acts of adoration arise naturally from your heart. This does not mean that you will always feel like praising. In truth, this does not matter. When your relationship with God is deep and lasting, praise comes no matter what you are experiencing because how you feel does not change who God is in your life.

Praise Is a Conscious Choice

Praise is an act of your will. When you offer God true praise, you make a conscious decision to commend, approve, and glorify Him. Praise, therefore, is not based on your emotions or feelings. You don't have to feel great or even good or okay—to praise the Lord. Despite the many things in your life that may seem to be wrong, praise is your conscious choice because you know that God is the answer to your problems. As long as He is in charge, things will get better. Your intimate fellowship with Him makes this difference. You can focus on what is right—God and His goodness to you—no matter what else is wrong.

This attitude is quite evident in Psalm 42, where the psalmist laments that his life is not like it once was when he went to the house of the Lord with great joy. His body hurts. Tears are his lot now instead of music and laughter. He even fears that God has forgotten him, so long has it been since he felt God's presence. Yet this hurting, despairing man makes a conscious choice. He exercises his will and chooses to remember God and His goodness. Notwithstanding his misery and his sorrow, the psalmist gives himself a lecture. He says, "Soul, why are you so upset? Why are you sulking and fretting as though you have no hope? Don't give up! Put your hope in God. He has not given up, even if you have. So, stop dwelling on everything that's wrong and start thinking about all that's right. Remember the friendship we've enjoyed with God. Recall His many acts of kindness to us. The difficult place we're in right now isn't the end of the story. I'm still going to praise Him, my Savior and my God." (See Psalm 42.)

Perhaps you are carrying a heavy load right now. You are going through some of the toughest times humans experience. Don't let your troubles keep you from praising the Lord. I know that you may feel like you are facing hardships few others have had to face, or that you have lost hope that your circumstances will ever change. This is precisely the time, dear friend, that God asks you to praise Him. He knows that you are hurting. He also knows that things won't always be the way they now are. In fact, He's waiting to act on your behalf, but He needs you to provide a dwelling place for Him, an altar in your life where He can show up. Praise is that altar.

Praise Is a Willing Sacrifice

Biblical expressions of praise often include the word *will*.

The Lord is my strength and my song; He has become my salvation. He is my God, and I *will* praise Him, my father's God, and I *will* exalt Him (Exodus 15:2).

I *will* give thanks to the Lord because of His righteousness and *will* sing praise to the name of the Lord Most High (Psalm 7:17).

I *will* sing to the Lord, for He has been good to me (Psalm 13:6).

> **The Lord is my strength and my shield; my heart trusts in Him, and I am helped. My heart leaps for joy and I *will* give thanks to Him in song** (Psalm 28:7).

Although "*will*" can indicate a future time, it can also speak of a conscious choice. In other words: "I am determined to praise God." This is what the Scriptures call a sacrifice or offering of praise.

> **I will sacrifice a freewill offering to You; I will praise Your name, O Lord, for it is good** (Psalm 54:6).

> **Through Jesus, therefore, let us continually offer to God a sacrifice of praise—the fruit of lips that confess His name** (Hebrews 13:15).

Praise becomes a sacrifice when you offer your praise to God just because He deserves it and asks you to do it. You may not feel like praising Him, and in truth, it may be quite difficult for you to look beyond the difficulties in your life. Yet, when you choose to open your lips and speak forth your adoration, gratitude, and thanksgiving to God, you please Him.

Truly, you can always give the Lord some sacrifice. No, you probably won't bring God a lamb, a sheep, or a goat as God's people did in the Tabernacle and the Temple. This does not free you, however, from the responsibility of bringing Him a gift when you come to worship Him. Praise from an obedient heart is the gift that pleases God the most. You may not have anything else to bring Him, but you can always give Him this sacrifice of praise.

Notice that Hebrews calls this "the fruit of our lips." Fruit speaks of a harvest. Farmers will tell you that bringing in the crops is hard work. Sometimes praise requires the same effort. Instead of calling people and waiting for them to minister to you when you are having a hard time, why don't you go ahead and have your own praise service. Sacrifice your hurt feelings, your financial problems, or your troubles with your boss or your wife or your son or daughter on the altar of praise. Make it your conscious choice to lay aside all that pulls you down or makes you afraid or causes you to feel like giving up, and open your mouth and talk to God. Tell Him how wonderful He is. Tell Him how thankful you are that He is in your life. Tell Him that you are glad He is on your side. Tell Him that He is worth more to you than everything else in the world.

This sacrifice of praise won't cost you any money, but it will cost you your self-centeredness and your natural tendency to dwell on whatever is wrong in your life. Giving God your sacrifice of praise means that you choose to dwell on Him instead of yourself. Your mouth is filled with all that is good in your life instead of everything that is bad. This sacrifice can never be forced from you by someone else. Oh, you may sing or raise your hands because someone tells you to, but outward show is not inward praise. A sacrifice of praise comes from inside you. It is your will taking control over your emotions and doing what God wants and empowers you to do.

The Book of Leviticus says it this way,

When you sacrifice a thank offering to the Lord, sacrifice it in such a way that it will be accepted on your behalf (Leviticus 22:29).

The King James Version ends the verse with these words: "Offer it at your own will." The sacrifice that is pleasing to God is what you give from your heart despite what you are feeling or what your cirumstances are. Somehow, you find the power in the midst of your difficulty to praise the Lord with what little strength you have. I don't know about you, but I prefer to praise with whatever strength I have left in hard times, rather than to complain.

> *P*raise given with whatever strength you have, however limited, is a sacrifice pleasing to God.

Complaining accomplishes nothing more than to further drain our strength. Praise brings the Lord into our thoughts, thereby lifting us above whatever is causing our struggle. Celebrating God by focusing on Him instead of us is truly the essence of praise. When we do this, God takes our sacrifice and blesses us.

So, don't wait for things to go right before you start praising God. Start praising the Lord, and things will go right. After days, weeks, and even months of this sacrifice of praise, you will find that you naturally find many things for which to praise Him. After all, He is deserving of every word of commendation, confidence, approval, good report, and honor you can give Him. The more you notice Him and His benefits to you, the more He will bless you and give you more reasons to praise Him.

Praise Is an Expression of Faith

Faith without deeds (works) is dead (see Jas. 2:17). Likewise, praise that is in the heart but is not expressed is dead. Therefore, faith is the highest act of praise, and praise is the highest form of faith. Both are expressions of agreement with God. When you have faith, you hold to His promises no matter what you see at the moment. When you praise Him, you proclaim what you know to be true despite the evidence to the contrary.

Think of Abraham when he tied Isaac to that altar on Mount Moriah. (See Genesis chapter 22.) I'm sure Abraham wasn't singing, dancing, and praising God in a festive way. Most likely his heart was quite heavy. Yet, the very act of placing Isaac on that altar was an act of praise. Why? Abraham was expressing his trust in God and his confidence that somehow everything would come out right. After all, not only had God given Isaac to Abraham and his wife, Sarah, when they were quite late in years; He had also promised that Abraham would have more descendants than the sands of the sea. Moreover, those grandchildren, great-grandchildren, and great-great-grandchildren were to come through Isaac, the son of promise, not through Ishmael. So either God would provide another sacrifice in the place of Isaac or He would somehow restore Isaac to Abraham after the sacrifice. In either case, Abraham was willing to trust God to keep His covenant and the promises that went with it.

An attitude of faith in the midst of hard times is always at the core of sacrificial praise because it is based in the assurance that anything is possible with God. What may be impossible for man is not beyond the reaches of God simply because of who He is. So praise that clings to who God is rather than to what we human beings see or do is a fundamental expression of faith. It is saying, "I don't know what You are doing, why You are doing it, or how this whole thing is going to end up, but I trust You, God. I know You will be faithful to me. You will never abandon me. Therefore, I'm going to obey You in as much as I understand to do. The rest is up to You. I do this because You are my God and my Savior. All I have, am, and ever hope to be is Yours." Such praise frees God to work in our lives.

> *P*raise is giving God all that is His due and giving Him room in our life to do all He wants to do.

❖ **PRINCIPLES** ❖

1. To praise means to commend, to approve, to give a favorable judgment, to glorify, and to esteem.

2. Praising God by commendation means that we entrust ourselves to His care and recommend that others do the same.

3. Praising God by approval means that we have a favorable opinion of God, which we tell Him and others.

4. Praising by giving God glory means that we honor Him and express our admiration for Him.

5. Praise turns the focus of our life from us to God.

6. Before we can consistently praise God, we must get close enough to Him to see His true nature and character.

7. Praise is a conscious choice, an act of our will.

8. A sacrifice of praise is the praise we give God from obedience despite how we feel.

Chapter 6

When Are We to Praise God?

**God is worthy of our praise all day,
every day, no matter what kind of a day it is.**

Perhaps you've heard the saying that there are two times to praise the Lord: when you feel like it, and when you don't. Any other time you don't have to praise Him. The implication is that you are to praise the Lord at all times. This is certainly the message of the psalmist:

I will extol the Lord at all times; His praise will always [continually, KJV] **be on my lips** (Psalm 34:1).

Therefore, praise is to be an everyday part of your life. No matter what's happening—whether you are having low moments or high moments—your focus is to stay on God.

In the Best of Times and the Worst of Times

In other words, God is worthy of your praise in the best of times, the worst of times, and all the mundane moments in between.

In the Best of Times

King David dreamed of building a permanent house for the Lord to replace the mobile Tabernacle that had housed the Ark of the Covenant since the days of Moses. The prophet Nathan had even put his stamp of approval on David's plans. Then the word of the Lord came to Nathan at night,

> **Go and tell My servant David, "This is what the Lord says: You are not the one to build Me a house to dwell in. I have not dwelt in a house from the day I brought Israel up out of Egypt to this day....did I ever say to any of their leaders whom I commanded to shepherd My people, 'Why have you not built Me a house of cedar?' " Now then, tell My servant David, "This is what the Lord Almighty says: I took you from the pasture and from following the flock, to be ruler over My people Israel. I have been with you wherever you have gone, and I have cut off all your enemies from before you. Now I will make your name like the names of the greatest men of the earth. And I will provide a place for My people Israel....I will also subdue all your enemies. I declare to you that the Lord will build a house for you: When your days are over and you go to be with your fathers, I will raise up your offspring to succeed you, one of your own sons, and I will establish his kingdom. He is the one who will build a house for Me, and I will establish his throne forever. I will be his father, and he will be My son....I will set him over My house and My kingdom forever; his throne will be established forever"** (1 Chronicles 17:4-14).

Wow! What a promise! God was giving David a house instead of David giving God a house. Isn't this just like our God? We plan something great and God does something even better. True, David didn't get to build God's house—his son Solomon did—yet David was so overcome with gratitude to God after hearing Nathan's report that he had his own little praise session:

There is no one like You, O Lord, and there is no God but You....You made Your people Israel Your very own forever, and You, O Lord, have become their God. And now, Lord, let the promise You have made concerning Your servant and his house be established forever. Do as You promised, so that it will be established and that Your name will be great forever (1 Chronicles 17:20-24a).

Sometime later, David gave gold and silver for the building of the Temple and asked who would join him in providing for God's house. The leaders of Israel gave willingly and the people rejoiced because of their generous giving. King David, overjoyed by the response of the people, again praised the Lord:

Then David said to the whole assembly, "Praise the Lord your God." So they all praised the Lord, the God of their fathers; they bowed low and fell prostrate before the Lord and the king. The next day they made sacrifices to the Lord and presented burnt offerings to Him (1 Chronicles 29:20-21a).

At some point in the praise and worship, God's presence must have come to His people, for the next verse says, "They ate and drank with great joy in the presence of the Lord that day" (1 Chron. 29:22a). Then they acknowledged Solomon as king.

David's world was certainly right that day. The leaders of the people had given generously for the building of the Temple and had acclaimed Solomon as king. Then God's presence had come, a joy David knew and loved above all else!

Remember, however, that this high was not a chance occurrence. I have to believe that God's coming in the midst of His people was prompted by not only the praise of David and the people but also David's lifestyle of praise. David never took God's goodness to him for granted. Repeatedly he told God how good He was and how grateful he, David, was for God's many blessings to him.

We would do well to follow David's example. Yes, we may praise God for a specific blessing, but few of us have developed a lifetime pattern of seeing all the good in our life as gifts from the hand of God. Praising God in the good times—of which there are many more than most of us admit—is an essential ingredient of our praise.

In the Worst of Times

Paul and Silas, on the other hand, were suffering one of life's low moments. For many days they had been followed by a slave girl who had a spirit that enabled her to tell fortunes. Day after day she had shouted, "These men are servants of the Most High God, who are telling you the way to be saved" (Acts 16:17b). Finally, having had enough of this, Paul commanded the spirit in the name of Jesus to leave the girl, which it did. The girl's owners, incensed by their loss of income, then stirred up the crowd and the leaders of the city until Paul and Silas were stripped, beaten, and thrown into jail, where their feet were placed in stocks.

What would most of us have done in such circumstances? We probably would have moaned and groaned about how unfair the events of the day had been. What did Paul and Silas do? They didn't start complaining about the darkness, the slimy moss on the walls, the stench of the urine in the hole where they had been thrown, or the rats they could hear and feel. Instead, Paul said, "Silas, let's sing." They spent the night praying and singing to the Lord—and not in a quiet, subdued manner, either. Their worship service was loud enough for the other prisoners to hear it.

Suddenly God entered the jail through an earthquake and the cell was too small for God to sit down. This is when the doors flew open and the chains dropped to the ground—and not just the chains that had held Paul and Silas in the stocks, either. When God moved in, things changed in that whole jail! (See Acts chapter 16.)

What a story! I'm sure that Paul and Silas' wounds hurt. They could have had quite a pity party. Yet, this was not their response because not only did they recognize their problem, they also knew that God was up to dealing with it. Therefore, they did the one thing that would get God's presence into that urine-soaked cell with them. They had a prayer and praise session.

I wonder what kind of prison you are in or what problem threatens to defeat you. It's easy to complain when you are faced with things that frighten you or circumstances that never seem to get better. Nevertheless, if you want God to come into your cell, you must resist the temptation to grumble, murmur, and complain. You have to make the decision to praise Him instead.

Just look beyond your feelings, your fears, and your circumstances to God. Praise Him for whatever goodness you have enjoyed from His hand, however small or insignificant it may seem to be. Instead of recalling everything that is wrong in your life, remember everything that is right.

If you will do this—if you will consciously choose to trust God and to proclaim His goodness to you—the Lion from the tribe of praise will show up and He will shatter your prison. Not only this, He'll loosen your chains and dispel your darkness too. No, you may not feel the earth tremble beneath your feet or see doors fly open, but you will find that your attitude and your outlook change as your praise brings His presence into your life. Just try it. Start small if you have to, but start somewhere. Find something in your life to praise God for, then open your mouth and create a place for Him to sit with you. You just might be surprised by what He does!

In the Mundane, In-Between Times

Don't think, however, that you have to be on the mountaintop or in the valley to have your own private praise session. Oftentimes the normal days of our life are the hardest times to praise God because there's nothing in particular to draw our attention to Him. This is why we must get into the habit of praising the Lord. Most of us have habits of murmuring. What would our life be like if we used that same energy to praise God? How might our days go if we turned our attention to Him instead of the ball game or the advertisements or the latest bestseller?

David talked to himself about God all the time. I don't think we have practiced that enough. We like to sing, "Bless the Lord, O my soul" (Ps. 103:1a KJV), but how often do we really do it? In truth, this phrase is a command to our soul to praise the Lord.

Your soul is your whole self: your will, your emotions, and your intellect. (See Genesis 2:7 KJV.) Therefore, if you are telling your soul to praise God, in reality you are commanding your body to respond to all three.

In other words, you first give yourself a talking to and take control over your will, your emotions, and your intellect. Then, once all three are focused on God and attentive to Him, your body acts in accordance with the instructions it receives from them. This is why you can still praise God when your will is indifferent, your emotions are blah, or your mind is bored. You body responds with praise because your will, your emotions, and your intellect—under your concious and attentive control—tell it to do so.

We think we have to have something great in our life before we can praise the Lord. This is a lie! David praised the Lord day in and day out. Whether he messed up or had just won a battle, he talked with God about it. He didn't need some special reason to sing, shout, or dance his adoration. He just did it all the time—even when things were boring and mundane.

You too must develop an attitude where praise becomes your protection all the time as you bring God around you. Whether you are typing a letter, loading a truck, taking care of children, or cleaning the house, just keep making melody to the Lord. Sometimes you might be humming a tune. Other times you may need to praise God in your mind. Whatever you are doing, you are just going through the whole day with God. Don't wait for something special to happen. Instead, make sure that God is with you every day and all day as you keep Him with you through your praise. Then, no matter what happens in your life, God is there to handle it.

> *P*raise is a day in, day out, responsibility.

Every Day and All Day

In Public and in Private

Some of us wait until church on Sunday before we praise God, and even then we don't come with praise and thanksgiving in our heart. Instead we come with our bad feelings and wait for some one to make us feel better.

Maybe you were up all night with the baby, you had a spat with your husband over breakfast, or your kids acted up in the car on the way to church. Whatever the reason, you come to church in a bad mood.

The apostle Paul instructs us to have a quite different attitude and disposition:

> **Speak to one another with psalms, hymns and spiritual songs. Sing and make music in your heart to the Lord, always giving thanks to God the Father for everything, in the name of our Lord Jesus Christ** (Ephesians 5:19-20).

This means that before you get to church, you are supposed to be praising God. Even before you get into the car, you are supposed to have had your own private praise service so that when you get with the rest of God's family, you are ready to ascend into God's presence with everybody else.

In essence, when you prepare in private for public praise, you don't need a worship leader to make you feel like praising God. Yes, there is a place for worship leaders in our corporate worship, but it is not their job to make you feel good enough to tell your Daddy how great He is.

> **I**t is not the job of the worship leader to inspire you to praise God.

If you have been talking to your own soul throughout the week the way you are supposed to be, you won't need anyone to get your attention and stir you up. You will already be eager and ready to go. In fact, you will be like David, who said,

> **I was glad when they said unto me, Let us go into the house of the Lord** (Psalm 122:1 KJV).

David rejoiced when the doors of God's house were open and he could go in. He was excited to worship with God's people. The same should be true for you. Your worship in private throughout the week should prepare you for Sunday worship with your brothers and sisters in Christ.

In essence, all of us are worship leaders because we are temples of the Lord (see 1 Cor. 3:16-17; 6:19). What we do in our own house affects what we do with everybody else. When we sanctify our house through righteous praise at home, we are then ready to sanctify the whole place when we come together.

Therefore, be careful not to come expecting something great in your public praise and worship if you haven't had an individual meeting with God first. Praise in your private life is what brings power and authority to your public experience.

David had no problem dealing with Goliath because he had a worship service behind the mountain before he went out to meet the enemy. His instructions and encouragement from God gave him the courage he needed to fight a man who was nine to ten feet tall. (See First Samuel chapter 17.) Moreover, David's pattern of private worship had given him the opportunity to see God's work on his behalf in the past. Therefore, he had the confidence to trust God again in these new circumstances.

Few of us operate from this perspective. If we functioned as David did, we would have a worship service at home, before we go to the bank to get a loan. Most of go for the loan first and cry to God if we don't get it. On the other hand, if the loan comes through, we praise God for the moment, then go back to life as usual.

I'm telling you, friends, your life would be quite different if you praised God before you met a challenge. Just try it. Have a private worship service in your home before you go to work. Put on some music that draws you into praise and worship, then spend some time with God before you walk out the door. Don't listen to the news before you go to work. Listen to God. Then He will fill your day with Himself because you started your day with Him.

> **Listen to God, not the news, before you leave your house in the morning.**

Many times the Lord works all day to get into your life because you didn't give Him the day in the beginning. He watches you go through your struggles and says, "My goodness! How I wish I could get into your day, but there's no place for Me to sit. You haven't praised Me, so there's no place for My presence to be enthroned."

Directly to God and Indirectly to Others

Praise is how we make room for God in our life. Sometimes our praise is offered directly to God, which is probably what we are most familiar with. We magnify and extol Him by speaking or singing our praise to Him as David did in Psalm 9:

> **I will praise You, O Lord, with all my heart; I will tell of all Your wonders. I will be glad and rejoice in You; I will sing praise to Your name, O Most High** (Psalm 9:1-2).

Not all our praise is to be direct, however. God also wants us to praise Him indirectly. This happens when we commend God and express our approval of Him to others.

God wants you to share with others what He is doing in your life. No matter how insignificant His activity in your life may seem to be to you, talk about it. Announce to your friends, family, and coworkers how He has sustained you and brought you through a difficult time. Testify to God's goodness and to what He has been doing for you. This is how He receives glory and honor.

Most of us tell people about our problems, complaints, dislikes, and misunderstandings. We are much more likely to murmur and clamor than to speak of the Lord's goodness to us. How sad! We are no different from the children of Israel who murmured their way through the wilderness and failed to recognize God's blessings and to give Him credit for everything He had done for them. Indeed, they were so disgruntled that they wanted to go back to Egypt, the land of their slavery!

God doesn't want you to have such an attitude. He wants you to see and proclaim the difference He has made in your life. David, again, is a good example of a man who did this. (No wonder God saw him as a man after His heart!) His praise was contagious because he wasn't content to praise God by himself. When he went to the Tabernacle, he wanted everybody else to praise God too.

> **I will extol the Lord at all times; His praise will always be on my lips. My soul will boast in the Lord; let the afflicted hear and rejoice. Glorify the Lord with me; let**

us exalt His name together. I sought the Lord, and He answered me; He delivered me from all my fears. Those who look to Him are radiant; their faces are never covered with shame. This poor man called, and the Lord heard him; He saved him out of all his troubles (Psalm 34:1-6).

David wanted everybody to know what God had done for him, and he wasn't shy about asking others to join Him in glorifying and exalting God.

We readily gossip about everything else. Now it's time that we gossip about the Lord's doings in our lives: "Did you hear what God did for so-and-so? He's just telling everyone—and he's telling them to tell even more people!"

Please stop reading a moment and really think about this. Wouldn't it be great if every time we saw each other we shared something good of what the Lord has done for us? How our conversation and our attitudes would change! Surely we would see even more of God's activity, since when we praise Him to others, He becomes excited to do the same thing again, and even more!

Sing a New Song Every Day

This is what the Scriptures mean by singing a new song:

Sing to Him a new song; play skillfully, and shout for joy (Psalm 33:3).

Sing to the Lord a new song; sing to the Lord, all the earth (Psalm 96:1).

Praise the Lord. Sing to the Lord a new song, His praise in the assembly of the saints (Psalm 149:1).

Our new song is to be a song of all God has done for us. It is based in our experience with Him.

David did this on a regular basis. Because he was always seeing God at work in his life, his song came out of the latest thing God had done for him.

> **Sing to the Lord a new song, for He has done marvelous things; His right hand and His holy arm have worked salvation for Him** (Psalm 98:1).

> **I waited patiently for the Lord; He turned to me and heard my cry. He lifted me out of the slimy pit, out of the mud and mire; He set my feet on a rock and gave me a firm place to stand. He put a new song in my mouth, a hymn of praise to our God. Many will see and fear and put their trust in the Lord** (Psalm 40:1-3).

God wants such praise from you as well. He is tired of hearing the same old testimonies you have shared repeatedly. In fact, if you'll listen, you'll hear Him asking you, "Do you have to tell the same old story again? Haven't I done anything for you since that wonderful time?"

Truly, your most effective testimony is to brag to other people about what God has done for you this week. Tell people what He did just yesterday, or even this morning. Then your song will always be new.

> **Y**our most effective testimony is to brag about what God did for you this morning.

This is what the children of Israel did when God drowned Pharaoh and all his army. Moses started singing and his sister, Miriam, picked up a tambourine and led the women in a victory procession, singing and dancing before the Lord.

> **Then Moses and the Israelites sang this song to the Lord: "I will sing to the Lord, for He is highly exalted. The horse and its rider He has hurled into the sea. The Lord is my strength and my song; He has become my salvation. He**

is my God, and I will praise Him, my father's God, and I will exalt Him. The Lord is a warrior; the Lord is His name. Pharaoh's chariots and his army He has hurled into the sea. The best of Pharaoh's officers are drowned in the Red Sea. The deep waters have covered them; they sank to the depths like a stone. Your right hand, O Lord, was majestic in power. Your right hand, O Lord, shattered the enemy. In the greatness of Your majesty You threw down those who opposed You. You unleashed Your burning anger; it consumed them like stubble. By the blast of Your nostrils the waters piled up. The surging waters stood firm like a wall; the deep waters congealed in the heart of the sea. The enemy boasted, 'I will pursue, I will overtake them. I will divide the spoils; I will gorge myself on them. I will draw my sword and my hand will destroy them.' But You blew with Your breath, and the sea covered them. They sank like lead in the mighty waters. Who among the gods is like You, O Lord? Who is like You—majestic in holiness, awesome in glory, working wonders? You stretched out Your right hand and the earth swallowed them" (Exodus 15:1-12).

Do you see what the Israelites sang? Detail by detail, they told the story of what God had done for them. Indeed, they had a big celebration because they were certain that the events they had just witnessed were evidence of God's protection and of His love for them. Therefore, they weren't afraid or ashamed to sing and dance before Him or to pass the song on to their kids, who told their kids, who told their kids, until we read it ourselves today in the Bible.

This song and dance of praise is not an isolated incident. The Scriptures are filled with testimonies to the goodness and greatness of God. Indeed, you can tell what God did by what the people sang. Nevertheless, not all these testimonies are joyous. Some show that God's activity did not always bring celebration. Consider, for example, Psalm 137:

> **By the rivers of Babylon we sat and wept when we remembered Zion. There on the poplars we hung our harps, for there our captors asked us for songs, our tormentors demanded songs of joy; they said, "Sing us one of the songs of Zion!" How can we sing the songs of the Lord while in a foreign land?** (Psalm 137:1-4)

We see here that God's people had nothing to sing about because they hadn't seen God work in their life for a long time. Their disobedience had brought His judgment on them and had taken them into exile far away from Jerusalem and the Temple that was God's dwelling place. So they hung up their instruments and refused to sing.

This should not be true for you—unless, of course, you too are in exile because of persistent sin and iniquity in your life. You may sometimes want to recount those high points in your life when He really came through for you, but be careful you don't get hung up there. No new songs might lead people to believe that God hasn't done anything for you lately—and you know that's not true!

Every single day you should have a new song to sing before the Lord and to share with others. This is how it is with praisers. Songs just show up because God's presence comes and stays. His anointing flows naturally through those who have learned to see and testify to His goodness. These songs of the Lord don't have to be worked up because they flow from the present moment, from the intimate experiences between God and His people. Such praise also keeps and seals the reality of those times with Him.

Therefore, if you want God's presence in your life, learn to be a praiser. Don't keep silent about His many benefits. Make it your purpose to find something new to sing to the Lord about every day. No matter what your circumstances are, surely you can find at least one praiseworthy thing each day. Then, when God sees your gratitude toward Him and your habit of celebrating His goodness to you, He'll come and stay with you. He'll make every day a blessing as He enjoys your attention and takes pleasure in your joy in Him.

In essence, God wants you to be bragging about your heavenly Daddy all the time. If you aren't, it just may mean that He isn't your Father yet. You haven't made the connection. You haven't established the relationship.

When God becomes your Father, praise becomes a natural part of your life. You don't have to think about it. Praise just naturally flows from your lips because you are seeing your Daddy's handiwork all the time and you just can't help telling Him how thankful you are that He is in your life.

You are like a child who can't wait to hear his dad's special whistle when he comes home from work. When the child hears the whistle, it doesn't matter what he is doing, he has to see Dad as fast as he can. So, he runs and flings open the door. Then he clings to his father, talking the whole time about everything that has happened in his day.

This is the way it should be with you and God. It doesn't matter who else is around, or what they may be doing or thinking, when you sense the presence of your heavenly Daddy, you have eyes and ears for nothing and no one else. Your praise bubbles up from within you just because He is there. Times may be good; times may be bad. This does not change your relationship with your Daddy. Once you have found the secret dwelling place of God in the midst of your praise, you go to Him day in and day out because there is no place you would rather be. His presence has become your true home, the environment for which you were created.

> **P**raise is to be as natural and as common to you as breathing.

❖ PRINCIPLES ❖

1. You don't need a special reason to praise God.

2. Every moment of every day is a suitable time for praise.

3. A lifestyle of praise teaches you to see and trust God's work in your life.

4. Private praise prepares you for public praise and worship.

5. Private praise prepares you for public victory.

6. Praise in the beginning of the day gives God room to handle whatever comes your way in the rest of the day.

7. Praise may be both direct and indirect.

8. When you commend God to others, you are praising Him indirectly.

9. Complaining destroys the atmosphere created by praise.

10. Your new song every day keeps God's presence with you.

Chapter 7

How Are We to Praise God?

Be the concert. Don't just attend one.

Praising God has many forms, all of which have a common denominator: Praise is always extroverted. In other words, praise can always be seen or heard. It cannot be hidden or kept silent. Therefore, all expressions of praise must be vocal or in some other way outwardly expressed.

For the Hebrew people, this seemed to be easy. A study of the Old Testament shows that they were an emotional, expressive people. Maybe this is why God liked them. They were not afraid to openly show how they felt about God. Celebration and exhilaration were regularly part of their worship.

This is not, however, always the case for us. Some Christians seem to prefer to sit and soak in church rather than to be active participants. Such behavior is not true praise. Just as you cannot cheer on your favorite sports team without moving around and making some noise, so you cannot praise God calmly and quietly. This is not to say that quiet times of worship are not sometimes appropriate—particularly after the presence of God has become manifested among His people. Yet, praise must be declared or manifested in some way. Otherwise, it is not praise.

Unfortunately, some of us are so inhibited that we refuse to abandon ourselves to praise. We don't want to express it in an observable manner. To avoid this outward expression is to disobey God, since He specifically commands us to let the sound of our praise be heard:

> **Praise our God, O peoples, let the sound of His praise be heard** (Psalm 66:8).

Many people assume that this command refers to singing. Singing is not, however, the only form of biblical praise that can be heard. Shouting, clapping, laughter, singing and praying in the Spirit, and playing musical instruments are all expressions of praise that can be heard. We must be careful, therefore, that we do not exclude certain forms of praise simply because we are uncomfortable with them. Rather, we should seek to understand why we are uncomfortable and to make adjustments that will challenge our comfort zone. Otherwise, how can we fully proclaim the good tidings that are ours in Christ Jesus?

> **You who bring good tidings to Zion, go up on a high mountain. You who bring good tidings to Jerusalem, lift up your voice with a shout, lift it up, do not be afraid; say to the towns of Judah, "Here is your God!"** (Isaiah 40:9)

The King James Version uses the phrase, "lift up thy voice with strength..." in this verse. This certainly seems to indicate that our praise is to reveal a definite conviction and involvement. We are not to speak or sing in a timid manner, but with energy and assurance. When we are uncomfortable, it is difficult to be either assured or energetic. Therefore, we must challenge ourselves to go beyond the forms of praise we have always used.

This is not to say that our praise is to be showy for the sake of show. Quite the contrary is true. Our praise is to be genuine and authentic, arising out of our relationship with God. Therefore, our praise can reflect no more than is truly inside. If we have no passion in our heart for God, we should not be surprised when our praise lacks passion. The absence or presence of passion for God within us just naturally becomes evident in our expressions of love, adoration, and appreciation.

> *P*raise comes from our relationship with God.

On the other hand, some of us may find a particular form of praise difficult because we prefer to be entertained rather than to do the praising ourselves. We love to go to concerts where there is lots of energy and excitement, but we resist showing that same level of intensity in our praise on a Sunday morning.

Praise requires effort on our part. It is not something another person can do for us. Yes, a worship leader can make suggestions that may lead us into praise, but we must make the choice for ourselves as to whether or not we are going to praise God.

Some people are also uncomfortable during times of praise because they think they are too dignified to celebrate God with abandon. I remember one day after services when one of our members was holding the daughter of one of our pastors. She was content to stay with this person until she saw her daddy. Then she started kicking and pulling away until the woman who was holding her could not hold her any longer. Therefore, she put the child on the floor and watched her run.

People were talking and walking all around, but this little girl didn't care who else was in the room. She had seen her daddy, and he was her sole focus. She also was unconcerned that her dress was in the air and she was showing her underwear.

Such abandonment is what the Lord wants from us. Often we become self-conscious because we are not God conscious. Yes, we may be feeling poorly, or things in our life may seem to be falling apart, but this is precisely when we need to run to our Father. He is the only One who can heal us and put us together again. Whether we feel like it or not, we need to praise Him.

I want to make sure you understand what I just said. You *need* to praise God, and you *need* to do it with your whole being. Your need is more critical than your level of comfort. Whenever you relinquish your will and praise God however His Spirit leads you, you will find that His presence is the only place you want to be. It is also the only place where you can find everything you really need.

Ask anyone you know who is a praiser. He or she will soon tell you that God fills those who hunger for Him, and He gives righteousness to those who thirst for it. (See Matthew 5:6.)

Biblical Forms of Praise

Every form of praise contained in the Scriptures is an expression that the Church as a whole, and we as individual members, need to use. I know that some denominations, congregations, and pastors like to choose which expressions of biblical praise they will use, but this is certainly not God's intent. Our degree of comfort or the popularity of a particular form of praise does not change the fact that it is both commanded in the Bible and taught by example.

Singing

Sing to the Lord, you saints of His; praise His holy name (Psalm 30:4).

Sing for joy to God our strength; shout aloud to the God of Jacob! (Psalm 81:1)

Come, let us sing for joy to the Lord; let us shout aloud to the Rock of our salvation (Psalm 95:1).

Speak to one another with psalms, hymns and spiritual songs. Sing and make music in your heart to the Lord (Ephesians 5:19).

Let the word of Christ dwell in you richly as you teach and admonish one another with all wisdom, and as you sing psalms, hymns and spiritual songs with gratitude in your hearts to God (Colossians 3:16).

Singing is certainly the most common form of praise practiced today. In the Scriptures, singing was part of both private and public worship, as well as of celebrations following a victory God had won. Examples of these victory celebrations include the song of Moses following the drowning of Pharaoh's army (see Ex. 15), the singing of the Israelite women after David killed Goliath (see 1 Sam. 18:6), and the song of David after God delivered him from the hand of Saul (see 2 Sam. 22).

Shouting

May those who delight in my vindication shout for joy and gladness; may they always say, "The Lord be exalted, who delights in the well-being of His servant" (Psalm 35:27).

Shout for joy to the Lord, all the earth, burst into jubilant song with music (Psalm 98:4).

Shouting is a less common form of praise today than singing. Nonetheless, singing and shouting are commanded together in the Scriptures, and either word may be used to translate the same Hebrew verb, *ranan*. Therefore, shouting and loud singing are to be companions in our praise. Together they express joy and exultation, as is seen following the consecration of Aaron and his sons, when the fire fell from God's presence and consumed the sacrifices (see Lev. 9:24). The people's rejoicing is described as shouting.

Making a Joyful Noise (So It Can Be Heard)

> **Praise our God, O peoples, let the sound of His praise be heard** (Psalm 66:8).

> **Make a joyful noise unto the Lord, all the earth: make a loud noise, and rejoice, and sing praise. Sing unto the Lord with the harp; with the harp, and the voice of a psalm. With trumpets and sound of cornet make a joyful noise before the Lord, the King** (Psalm 98:4-6 KJV).

There's a place for triumphant celebration and loud worship. God is not nervous, so we can make noise. Indeed, He evidently enjoys it, for the Bible includes commands that we make a joyful noise before Him. This joyful noise may be singing, shouting, or some other audible form of praise.

Laughter

> **When the Lord brought back the captives to Zion, we were like men who dreamed. Our mouths were filled with laughter, our tongues with songs of joy. Then it was said among the nations, "The Lord has done great things for them." The Lord has done great things for us, and we are filled with joy** (Psalm 126:1-3).

> **He will yet fill your mouth with laughter and your lips with shouts of joy** (Job 8:21).

This form of praise is rarely used today and is even treated with suspicion by some people. Yet, the Bible tells us to rejoice with laughter. Psalm chapter 126, in particular, paints a lovely picture of laughing with delight over God's goodness in bringing His people back from exile. It is an expression of pure joy and wonder following a difficult season. The same seems to be true in Job, where joy and laughter are also used in a parallel form.

Thanksgiving

> **With praise and thanksgiving they sang to the Lord: "He is good; His love to Israel endures forever"** (Ezra 3:11a).

> **I will praise God's name in song and glorify Him with thanksgiving** (Psalm 69:30).

> **Enter His gates with thanksgiving and His courts with praise; give thanks to Him and praise His name** (Psalm 100:4).

> **Speak to one another with psalms, hymns and spiritual songs. Sing and make music in your heart to the Lord, always giving thanks to God the Father for everything, in the name of our Lord Jesus Christ** (Ephesians 5:19-20).

Thanksgiving and praise are often used in parallel constructions in the Scriptures, as is evident in the verses quoted above. In particular, they seem to be paired in public worship. The Book of Nehemiah, where it states that the priests were to stand opposite each other and perform an antiphonal form of praise and thanksgiving (see Neh. 12:24), provides an example of this. Ezra 3:11, Psalm 69, and Ephesians 5:19-20 also seem to indicate that thanksgiving incorporated singing.

Standing

> **At that time the Lord set apart the tribe of Levi to carry the ark of the covenant of the Lord, to stand before the Lord to minister and to pronounce blessings in His name, as they still do today** (Deuteronomy 10:8).

> **They were also to stand every morning to thank and praise the Lord. They were to do the same in the evening** (1 Chronicles 23:30).

> And the Levites...said: "Stand up and praise the Lord your God, who is from everlasting to everlasting." "Blessed be Your glorious name, and may it be exalted above all blessing and praise" (Nehemiah 9:5).

> Behold, bless ye the Lord, all ye servants of the Lord, which by night stand in the house of the Lord (Psalm 134:1 KJV).

Standing is a bit more common form of praise than some are, but we need to increase our times of standing before the Lord in worship. Sometimes after we stand for a while, we become self-conscious and think we are getting tired. Even then we should remain on our feet because standing is an act of honor. We stand in worship because it shows our respect for God.

Kneeling

> Come, let us bow down in worship, let us kneel before the Lord our Maker (Psalm 95:6).

> For this reason I kneel before the Father (Ephesians 3:14).

> That at the name of Jesus every knee should bow, in heaven and on earth and under the earth, and every tongue confess that Jesus Christ is Lord, to the glory of God the Father (Philippians 2:10-11).

Kneeling is a form of both humility and honor in our praise and worship. It shows our recognition that God is the Lord and we are His people. Some people still kneel for prayer, but in many denominations and congregations, kneeling is no longer practiced at all. Reinstating kneeling to our worship services would do much to restore the sense of reverence that we are sometimes missing.

Clapping Our Hands

> Clap your hands, all you nations; shout to God with cries of joy (Psalm 47:1).

Let the rivers clap their hands, let the mountains sing together for joy (Psalm 98:8).

You will go out in joy and be led forth in peace; the mountains and hills will burst into song before you, and all the trees of the field will clap their hands (Isaiah 55:12).

Clapping is a show of approval and appreciation. Yet, many churches don't encourage people to clap their hands to the Lord. Those who omit clapping from their praise do themselves harm because God is the One who determines how we should praise Him.

Moreover, clapping has benefits that we don't fully understand. Studies done in Japan over the last thousand years have shown that our hands and feet contain nerves that attach to every organ in our body. When we walk, we are therefore stimulating all our organs and giving them life.

The same is true for our hands. Maybe this is why God commands us to praise Him with clapping. He knows that as we clap, the nerves in our palms and fingers stimulate our whole body, bringing us life. Thus, when God says, "Clap your hands," He's really saying, "Get life." How like our God to give us commands regarding praise that not only bring honor to Him but also benefit us in ways beyond the blessings of obedience.

If you don't believe me, try this sometime. When you are getting drowsy in the middle of the day, or you have trouble getting up in the morning, start clapping. You will feel your whole body wake up and start to work again.

Dancing

Let them praise His name with dancing and make music to Him with tambourine and harp (Psalm 149:3).

> **Praise Him with tambourine and dancing, praise Him with the strings and flute** (Psalm 150:4).

> **The Lord your God is with you, He is mighty to save. He will take great delight in you, He will quiet you with His love, He will rejoice** [joy, KJV] **over you with singing** (Zephaniah 3:17).

Few congregations use dance in worship, and some folks actually disapprove of it, but dancing before the Lord is scriptural. In truth, Psalm 149:3 specifically admonishes us to let people praise Him with dance. Sometimes this is the only form of praise that can adequately express the intense joy and longing that well up inside us. We know we must move physically to release our love and devotion to the Lord.

Certainly dancing must be done decently and in order. Yet, we must be careful not to limit such expression because we do not believe in it or do not understand it. Dancing is both an acceptable and essential part of our worship.

At times, our dancing may even become boisterous as we leap and show great joy. This was surely true for Miriam and the other women in Exodus 15 who celebrated God's victory with timbrel and dance. It was also true of Jesus when the disciples He had sent out two by two came back telling of all they had seen and done. Luke 10:21 (KJV) says that Jesus "rejoiced in spirit." The Greek word that is translated here *rejoice* means to "jump for joy" (Strong's, G21). In a similar manner, the word *giyl* (Strong's, H1523), used in Zephaniah to speak of God's rejoicing over us, means "to spin under the influence of a violent emotion, i.e. usually rejoice."

I wonder how often the Lord is dancing in the Spirit but we are sitting still. He is having so much fun, but He is watching us and wondering why we don't dance too. If the joy of the Lord is truly in our heart, it will sometimes show up in our feet!

Uplifted Hands

I will praise You as long as I live, and in Your name I will lift up my hands (Psalm 63:4).

Lift up Your hands in the sanctuary and praise the Lord (Psalm 134:2).

I want men everywhere to lift up holy hands in prayer, without anger or disputing (1 Timothy 2:8).

Many of us sing about praising God with uplifted hands, but we seldom do it. Yet, we see here that we are commanded to lift our hands in God's sanctuary. The sanctuary is where we come to worship. It's God's holy dwelling place. Therefore, if God says to lift holy hands, we'd better do it. If we don't obey this command of the Lord, we can't expect Him to keep His promises to us, since He is holy and cannot lie. Our obedience is what opens God's hands to give us what He has promised.

Therefore, our praise must meet God's requirements all the time. We can't choose when and where we will lift our hands or do any of the other forms of praise. Obedience requires that we follow the leading of God's Spirit wherever we are and whenever He prompts us to praise.

This is what obedience is. It's going against our own will to fulfill the will of another; it is submitting our desires to the desires of someone else. In essence, we object to our own personal wishes so we can submit to the wishes of another. Praising with uplifted hands is thus a matter of obedience, not of personal preference.

Speaking and Singing in Tongues

For they heard them speaking in tongues and praising God (Acts 10:46a).

> **For anyone who speaks in a tongue does not speak to men but to God. Indeed, no one understands him; he utters mysteries with his spirit** (1 Corinthians 14:2).

> **So what shall I do? I will pray with my spirit, but I will also pray with my mind; I will sing with my spirit, but I will also sing with my mind** (1 Corinthians 14:15).

Speaking in tongues is a natural part of praise. It is speaking to God in the spirit. We need to understand, however, that there are two kinds of tongues. The first kind is given to one member of the congregation during a worship service for the instruction and building up of the Body. It is to be heard by the rest of the congregation and must be followed by the gift of interpretation, which comes through prophetic utterance. The second kind of tongues, which is part of our individual praise and prayer, is spoken to God in public or in private for the building up of the faith of the individual believer. This tongues, which is a personal gift from the Lord to His beloved child, may also be used in worship.

Therefore, those who are not baptized in the Holy Spirit are missing an important part of praise and prayer. In essence, the Spirit assists God's people in praise and worship through tongues.

Making Music on Instruments

> **David and the whole house of Israel were celebrating with all their might before the Lord, with songs and with harps, lyres, tambourines, sistrums and cymbals** (2 Samuel 6:5).

> **Praise the Lord. Praise God in His sanctuary; praise Him in His mighty heavens. Praise Him for His acts of power; praise Him for His surpassing greatness. Praise Him with the sounding of the trumpet, praise Him with the harp and lyre, praise Him with tambourine and dancing, praise Him with the strings and flute, praise Him with the clash of cymbals, praise Him with**

resounding cymbals. Let everything that has breath praise the Lord. Praise the Lord (Psalm 150).

Psalm 150 in its entirety exhorts us to praise the Lord, and instruments are an important part of this praise. Instruments are not, however, to take over the praise and worship time. This is not God's intent. Praise through musical instruments isn't to be offered until after we have brought our sacrifice of thanksgiving and raised our voice in praise.

How We Praise Depends on How Well We Know the One We Praise

The characteristics of our praise to the Lord depends on the depth of our relationship with Him. If we have built an intimate, lasting friendship with Him and have become perceptive praisers, we can expect that all these forms of praise will be part of our experience. Should this not yet be our practice, we can start where we are and ask God to lead us into the less common forms. Those persons who sincerely desire to obey Him in praise will find that He soon answers their prayers.

In truth, the more we abandon ourselves to the work and leading of God's Spirit within us, the more we emulate the praise that is pictured in the Scriptures. And why should we not, since praise leads us to our heart's true home. There, as God's presence comes to us and stays with us, we discover the depths of joy and wonder reserved for those who wholly give themselves to the praise of God. Our praise is no longer governed by traditions or comfort zones. Instead, we find that we *need* every form of worship God has given

> **P**raise reveals on the outside what is happening on the inside.

us because no one form or expression can adequately reveal the love, adoration, and faith we feel inside. True praise shows forth in some observable manner our delight and our wonder that God has chosen us to be His children and even now draws us close to Him.

❖ PRINCIPLES ❖

1. Praise takes many forms but must always be visible or audible.

2. We cannot choose which forms of praise we want to use. We need to praise God with our whole being.

3. Nobody can praise God for us.

4. Biblical forms of praise include:

   - Singing
   - Shouting
   - Making a joyful noise
   - Laughter
   - Thanksgiving
   - Standing
   - Kneeling
   - Clapping
   - Dancing
   - Uplifted hands
   - Speaking and singing in tongues
   - Making music on instruments

Chapter 8

Why Are We to Praise God?

Praise brings God into your environment.

Why should you praise God? This is a good question. Does God have an ego problem so that He needs you to tell Him how great or good He is? Does God have fits of depression so that He needs you to encourage Him occasionally? Does God have an emotional problem that makes Him crave your praise and attention?

God Does Not Need Your Praise

No! God does not need your praise. He's the same yesterday, today, and forever (see Heb. 13:8). He isn't moved by what you say or do.

I used to think that I moved God when I praised Him. Therefore, I praised Him in a loud voice and with loud instruments. I thought if I praised God loudly, He would respond quickly. I found out, however, that God is not moved by me. He's the same whether or not I praise Him. He is not emotionally unstable so that my praise changes how He feels about Himself—or about me.

If God were moved by my praise—or by my lack of praise—I would be able to determine what kind of day God has. How absurd! If this were true, He would not be—indeed, could not be—the faithful, unchanging God He is. Instead, the quality of His day would depend on the quality of my praise.

> **G**od is the same whether or not you praise Him.

Why, then, if my praise does not move or change God, does change sometimes come because of praise? Whom does the praise affect?

Praise Affects You

God is the same all the time, but you are not. This is why you need the stability of God's unchanging presence to keep your world in balance. You need Somebody who is, and always will be, the same every day, all day.

Our days go up and down—sometimes higher, sometimes lower. This is never true for God. His days are always up. He's there all the time with the same attitude, the same perspective, and the same abilities. Consequently, His presence in your day is quite important.

When He is with you because you have created an atmosphere in which He can dwell, your day is a day of His making no matter what it holds—thus, the common saying, "Lord, help me to remember that there is nothing in this day that You and I can't handle together." In other words, God makes your day when you give it to Him at the start through praise.

So if you were just fired, say, "God, make my day," and invite Him to come to you through praise. Then He can turn your firing into a hiring. Likewise, if you wake up feeling ill, say, "God, make my day," and praise Him despite your illness. This gives Him the opportunity to get into your environment where He can touch and heal you.

In essence, no matter what is going on in your life, if you will invite God into your day through praise, He will fill your life with Himself. Then the words, "make my day," become more than a cute saying. They become reality as God takes the threads of your life and weaves His tapestry. This is why the apostle Paul could say,

> **P**raise invites God to "make your day."

> **And we know that in all things God works for the good of those who love Him, who have been called according to His purpose** (Romans 8:28).

When God's plans and purposes are worked out in your life, every day and all day becomes good.

Praise Puts God to Work

Praise also invites God to do more good things for you. In fact, He enjoys showing us that He is even greater than we imagined and much more capable than we have yet seen.

> **Now to Him who is able to do immeasurably more than all we ask or imagine, according to His power that is at work within us, to Him be glory in the church and in Christ Jesus throughout all generations, for ever and ever! Amen** (Ephesians 3:20-21).

I wonder, therefore, what our life would be like if we consistently attracted God through praise. What would our families, neighborhoods, and nations look like? Would counselors and social workers be out of work? Would the bars and clubs in our town be empty and our churches be full? Would divorce, abortion, and child abuse become scourges of the past? Would decent housing be available for everyone and would the streets of our cities be safe to walk at night?

Such scenarios may seem to be impossible, but God specializes in the impossible. There is no telling what is possible when He arrives and takes over.

Jehoshaphat, king of Judah, evidently knew this. When threatened by a vast army that struck terror in his heart, Jehoshaphat turned to God for help. He proclaimed a fast, called the people together, and had a praise session in front of the Temple.

God
specializes
in the
impossible.

> **Then Jehoshaphat stood up in the assembly of Judah and Jerusalem at the temple of the Lord in the front of the new courtyard and said: "O Lord, God of our fathers, are You not the God who is in heaven? You rule over all the kingdoms of the nations. Power and might are in Your hand, and no one can withstand You** (2 Chronicles 20:5-6).

Do you see what the king did? He bragged about God. He proclaimed that power and might are in God's hand, not man's. He testified to his faith that no one can withstand God. Then he reminded God what He had already done for His people and confirmed his faith that God was up to the job.

> **O our God, will You not judge them? For we have no power to face this vast army that is attacking us. We do not know what to do, but our eyes are upon You** (2 Chronicles 20:12).

"Tell us what to do, God. We're not doing anything until You tell us what we should do. We're just waiting here for You because You are our God and we trust You."

Praise, expectancy, and obedience. This was Jehoshaphat's response to the threat of war. This should be your response as well in the face of adversity, because praise is the secret to the power of God.

I know that some of you have little time for this "spiritual stuff" because your needs are practical needs. Indeed, I've heard people say, "Yeah, I appreciate all this praise and other things you are talking about, but let's become practical now. Let's be reasonable. All this spiritual stuff isn't going to pay my mortgage or get my boss to stop hassling me or get my kids to quit hanging with the wrong crowd or get my spouse to stop running around. I'm dealing with real issues here and I need real answers."

You are exactly right. You are dealing with real issues—issues that are every bit as threatening as the army that would soon be on Judah's doorstep. So maybe you had better deal with them the same way Jehoshaphat dealt with the Moabites and the Ammonites:

> **Early in the morning they left for the Desert of Tekoa. As they set out, Jehoshaphat stood and said, "Listen to me, Judah and people of Jerusalem! Have faith in the Lord your God and you will be upheld; have faith in His prophets and you will be successful." After consulting the people, Jehoshaphat appointed men to sing to the Lord and to praise Him for the splendor of His holiness as they went out at the head of the army, saying: "Give thanks to the Lord, for His love endures forever"** (2 Chronicles 20:20-21).

What did Jehoshaphat do? As he led his people into battle, he said, "Let's sing. I want you to thank God for His faithfulness and to celebrate His love. Tell Him how beautiful His holiness is."

This may appear to be an unreasonable response, but let's see how it worked out.

> **As they began to sing and praise, the Lord set ambushes against the men...who were invading Judah, and they were defeated. The men of Ammon and Moab rose up against the men from Mount Seir to destroy and annihilate them. After they finished slaughtering the men**

> from Seir, they helped to destroy one another. When
> the men of Judah came to the place that overlooks the
> desert and looked toward the vast army, they saw only
> dead bodies lying on the ground; no one had escaped
> (2 Chronicles 20:22-24).

Wow! Not one man from the attacking army escaped the vindication of God.

To understand what was so special about Judah's victory, you need to understand the significance of their praise. Those singers out in front of the army weren't just having a casual praise session. They were doing serious business because they were appealing to God's integrity. This is what "the splendor of God's holiness" (vs. 21) refers to. His holiness means that He can't do anything other than what He has promised. Therefore, the men at the head of the army were praising God as though the army coming at them was already dead! They were rejoicing in God's faithfulness before He had been faithful. Why could they do this? They believed that the One who had made the promise would do exactly what He had said:

> You will not have to fight this battle. Take up your posi-
> tions; stand firm and see the deliverance the Lord will
> give you, O Judah and Jerusalem. Do not be afraid; do
> not be discouraged. Go out to face them tomorrow, and
> the Lord will be with you (2 Chronicles 20:17).

The average person would have run from that approaching army. He would have sought some way to escape the coming destruction. This was not what Jehoshaphat did. His words to his people show just how different his response was:

> Listen to me, Judah and people of Jerusalem! Have faith
> in the Lord your God and you will be upheld; have faith
> in His prophets and you will be successful (2 Chronicles
> 20:20b).

A song of faith in the night is the highest form of praise. It shows that you believe God's word to you to be true, and you trust Him to fulfill it. You attract Him through praise because your praise shows that you have faith:

And without faith it is impossible to please God, because anyone who comes to Him must believe that He exists and that He rewards those who earnestly seek Him (Hebrews 11:6).

Faith pleases God. This is why, when the bulldozer is coming toward you and you begin to praise Him, God says, "I will deliver you from the hands of this enemy." He begins to work for you because He is pleased with your praise and the faith that enables it.

Praise Puts Flesh to Our Faith

Praise fixed firmly upon faith opens the door for God to work for you, in you, and through you. It allows Him to handle all the things in your life that you cannot. This was certainly true for one leper whom Jesus healed. The Gospel of Luke tells us that ten lepers begged Jesus for mercy, but only one returned to thank Him (see Lk. 17:17-19). Praise also followed the faith of the blind beggar who told Jesus that he wanted to see (Lk. 18:35-43).

So, what are you waiting for? You *need* to praise God in the midst of your problems, and you need to do it now. Your praise is what attracts God to you. It is what gets you into His presence.

- Praise Him because you believe in Him and want to please Him.

- Praise Him because you want to honor and obey Him.

- Praise Him because you know you cannot live apart from Him.

- Praise Him because you need Him every hour of every day to be truly human.

- Praise Him because there are circumstances, events, and relationships in your life that you don't know how to handle.

- Praise Him because He has made promises to you that have yet to be fulfilled.

- Praise Him because you are certain He will be faithful to fulfill all He has spoken to you.

- Praise Him because there's power in praise and you want to tap every bit of that power.

- Praise Him because His ultimate goal is that you will bask in His presence and eat at His table forevermore (see Ps. 23).

> **P**raise is your God-given privilege and responsibility.

Finally, if these aren't enough reasons why you should praise your God, praise Him simply because His presence is more important to you than anything and everything that's keeping you from praising Him.

❖ **PRINCIPLES** ❖

1. God does not need your praise.

2. Your praise does not change or affect Him.

3. Your praise changes and affects you.

4. Praise brings God into your day so He can handle whatever comes your way.

5. Praise turns impossibilities into victories.

6. Praise based on faith thanks God for what He will do, before He does it.

Chapter 9

The Progression of Praise

Praise takes you up the hill of the Lord.

As a boy tending his father's sheep, David spent many hours playing his harp and singing to the Lord. This evidently put a love in his heart both for God and for music. The Book of Psalms, the longest book in the Bible, records many of these songs and prayers that poured from David's heart. David's ability to praise God is no doubt the primary reason Israel enjoyed a prosperity and security during his years as king that were unequaled throughout the rest of Israel's history. David knew how to get close to God, and God's presence made a great difference in David's life.

God also makes a difference for us when He is near. Sadly, His manifest presence is often absent from our churches. We come to beautiful structures but we see no power because the Spirit of God is not active among us. This is due in large part because we do not know how to attract Him. We don't know how to build a throne where God can sit in the midst of His people. Oh, we may sing, dance, clap, and go through the rest of the forms and motions that characterize praise, yet we never experience the awesome reality of seeing God's presence manifest among His people.

Why is this? Is God reluctant to come to us? Could He who created man so He would have a family prefer to be apart from His children? Of course not! The reason for God's absence is certainly not a matter of disinterest on His part. Disinterest on our part is a much more likely possibility, or at least interest that is limited or short-lived because we do not understand what He wants in our praise.

Praise that reaches God takes us beyond the confinement of routines, yet actually follows a pattern or a progression, if you will. This pattern is seen in seven Hebrew words that are used in the Old Testament to describe praise. These seven are certainly not the only words used to command and exemplify praise, but they reveal the essence of what God-attracting praise entails. The first of these dimensions or portraits, as we will call them, is _todah_.

The Seven Dimensions or Portraits of Praise

Todah (Towdah)

Todah (Strong's, H8426; Vine's, "To Praise"), the first dimension of praise, occurs in the Old Testament 30 times. It is probably the most challenging of the dimensions because it is totally an act of the will. Literally, meaning "an extension of the hand," _todah_ is a noun form based on the primitive root _yadah_.

In modern Hebrew _todah_ is preserved as the regular word for "thanks." In the Bible, it is used in songs of worship and is translated as "praise" (see Ps. 42:4 KJV; 50:23 KJV; 56:12 KJV), "thanksgiving" (see Ps. 26:7 KJV; 50:14 KJV; 69:30; Is. 51:3), and "giving thanks" (see Neh. 12:27-38), with a particular emphasis on the concept of offering praise or thanksgiving as a sacrifice to God (see Ps. 50:14,23; 56:12; 107:22; 116:17; Jer. 17:26; 33:11; Amos 4:5). This concept of giving an offering or sacrifice to God is also seen in that *todah* is the word used to refer to the thank offerings presented in the Tabernacle (see Lev. 7:12-15; 2 Chron. 29:31; 33:16; Psalm 50:14,23; 56:12). *Todah* may also mean to "make confession" to God concerning sin (see Josh. 7:19; Ezra 10:11).

Thus, *todah* is the result of a conscious choice that takes us beyond our feelings and preferences. It causes us to praise God no matter what is going on in our life and no matter how uncomfortable we are with the forms of praise the Holy Spirit leads us into. In other words, *todah* is our sacrifice, our offering, that tells God we want Him and are willing to make an effort to be with Him.

Yadah

Yadah (Strong's, H3034; Vine's, "To Confess" and "To Praise"), the second dimension of praise, not surprisingly has some of the same meanings as *todah*. Literally, *yadah* means to use or hold out the hand, or to physically throw a stone or an arrow at or away from something (see Lam. 3:53; Jer. 50:14). In the Scriptures, it refers primarily to extending the hands in reverence or worship. Thus, *yadah* is the dimension of praise where you begin to take control over your body and your mind.

First used in the story of the birth of Judah, *yadah* is used primarily in the Book of Psalms. It is translated as to "praise" (see Gen. 29:35; Ps. 7:17; 9:1), to "give thanks" (see 2 Sam. 22:50; 1 Chron. 25:3; Ps. 18:49), to "thank" (see 1 Chron. 16:4; 23:30), and "thanksgiving" (see Neh. 11:17). Overlapping in meaning with other Hebrew words for praise, including *halal, yadah* is found in the Scriptures primarily in settings of public rituals and worship, particularly where the group of worshipers is renewing their relationship with God. Often this occurs in the context of reciting or celebrating God's acts of salvation and in glorifying His name. Rarely is *yadah* used in the context of individual worship.

Not surprisingly, this praise in public worship is also accompanied by man's recognition of his unworthiness to receive all

God's benefits. Thus, *yadah*, like *todah*, may have the meaning of making confession for sin. Hence it is translated "confess" or "confession" some 20 times in the Old Testament (see Lev. 5:5; 16:21; Num. 5:7; Ezra 10:1; Ps. 32:5; Prov. 28:13).

Halal

Halal (Strong's, H1984; Vine's, "To Praise"), the third dimension of praise, is derived from a primitive root that means, among other things, "to be clear," "to shine," "to make a show," "to boast," "to be (clamorously) foolish," "to rave."

In the Scriptures, in addition to "praise," *halal* is translated as "commend" (see Gen. 12:15 KJV; Prov. 12:8 KJV), "boast" (see 1 Kings 20:11; Ps. 10:3; 34:2; 97:7), "celebrate" (see Is. 38:18 KJV), "glory" (see 1 Chron. 16:10; Ps. 105:3; Is. 41:16), "exult" (see Is. 45:25), "sing praises" (see 2 Chron. 23:13), and "shine" (see Job 31:26 KJV; 41:18 KJV). Since *halal* is also translated "insane" (see 1 Sam. 21:13), or "fools" and "foolish" (see Job 12:17; Ps. 5:5 KJV; 73:3 KJV; Eccl. 2:2), it suggests a sense of foolishness or abandonment in praise. Therefore, some people won't praise God with *halal* because they are too dignified. They refuse to look even a little bit foolish in their celebration of God.

Found in the Old Testament more than 160 times, *halal* may also be used in the praise of people, but the more common usage is in praise of God—hence, the word *Hallelujah*, a Hebrew word from the same root, which is usually translated "Praise the Lord!"

Shabach

Shabach (Strong's, H7812) is the fourth dimension of praise. It means to "address in a loud voice," particularly with a sense of triumph. The words used to translate *shabach* include, "glory" and "glorify" (see 1 Chron. 16:35; Ps. 63:3; 106:47), "commend" (see Ps. 145:4; Eccl. 8:15), and "extol" (see Ps. 117:1; 147:12).

I wonder what would happen in our churches and our homes if we would truly glorify the Lord with a voice of triumph. Some churches are so quiet and dignified that *shabach* would no doubt shake them up.

When we address the Lord with a loud voice of triumph, we commend Him for His character and nature and command Him to fulfill all He has said He will do. We approach Him with *shabach* because we want Him to respond to our need.

Zamar

Zamar (Strong's, H2167; Vine's, "To Sing"), the fifth dimension of praise, is based on a primitive root that means "to touch the strings or parts of a musical instrument" with the sense of playing it or of making music that is accompanied by the voice. Thus, *zamar* has the connotation of celebration with song and music, and is often found in a parallel structure with *shir* (Strong's, H7891), another Hebrew word for *singing. Zamar* is translated as "sing" (see Ps. 27:6; 30:4; 108:3), "give praise" (see Ps. 57:7 KJV), "sing praises" (see 2 Sam. 22:50; Ps. 47:6; 68:32), "praise" (see Ps. 21:13), "make music" (see Ps. 33:2; 98:5), and "psalms" (see 1 Chron. 16:9 KJV; Ps. 105:2 KJV). *Zamar* also has the association of praising God with instruments (see Ps. 150) and through dance (see Ps. 149:3).

Please note that *zamar* is the fifth dimension, not the first. You don't start praise by making music, because music with instruments is to be an extension of your praise, not a creation of it. Praise starts with *todah* and *yadah*—thanksgiving—which may be given by everyone, since we all have breath.

Let everything that has breath praise the Lord. Praise the Lord (Psalm 150:6).

Perhaps our churches are devoid of God's power because we want to start with music, but God wants us to start with thanksgiving. This is not to say that thanksgiving may not be given through music, but we must be careful not to expect the musicians and worship leaders to do for us what we need to do for ourselves. Truly, we cannot praise God through the thanksgivings of another. Thanksgiving must come from our own grateful heart and be expressed by our own willing lips. This is the only way our celebration through music can be genuine. We have to know that we have something to celebrate before the celebration can happen. Thanksgiving reminds us whose we are and what He has done for us. This, then, is why we celebrate.

Barak

Barak (Strong's, H1288; Vine's, "To Bless"), the sixth portrait of praise, is a primitive root meaning, "to kneel." By implication, it also means, "to bless God," as in an act of adoration (see Ps. 95:6). *Barak* therefore carries with it a sense of hushed expectancy and often comes when the Holy Spirit begins to minister, filling the praise that has been offered. In this sense, *barak* is the beginning of God's response in worship. We stop and wait for God to do something.

Too often, we never reach this stage because we are so busy talking to God that we give Him little or no chance to speak to us. When we do this, we miss the prophecy, tongues, and words of wisdom, encouragement, and edification that He wants to give to us, His beloved children.

> *P*raise that reaches God requires listening as well as speaking.

While *barak* is often translated to "bless," particularly in the King James Version (see Gen. 9:26; Deut. 1:11; Jer. 4:2), other English translations use "praise" (see Gen. 24:48; Josh. 22:33; 1 Sam. 25:32; 1 Kings 10:9; Ps. 41:13) when referring to people blessing God, and "congratulate" (see 1 Kings 1:47) and "thank" (see Deut. 24:13) when referring to people blessing people. *Barak* is also used to refer to God's blessing on human beings (see Gen. 1:22; 9:1; Deut. 12:7; Ps. 45:2) and the things they do and need (see Ex. 23:25; Deut. 16:15), and of the blessings given by the priests in God's name (see Deut. 21:5). In a somewhat interesting counterpoint, *barak* is also used to refer to blasphemy or cursing against God (see 1 Kings 21:10,13; Job 1:5).

Tehillah

Tehillah (Strong's, H8416; Vine's, "To Praise") is the final dimension of praise. It is based on a root that means "laudation," especially as it refers to hymns (see Ps. 40:3), and it speaks of the praiseworthy quality of a person or thing. These songs from the heart and the spirit are given to each individual believer and cannot be learned or duplicated. They are unpremeditated utterances inspired by the Holy Spirit and as such are evidence that He is worshiping through us.

The apostle Paul refers to these types of songs when he writes to the Ephesian and Corinthian churches:

Speak to one another with psalms, hymns and spiritual songs. Sing and make music in your heart to the Lord, always giving thanks to God the Father for everything, in the name of our Lord Jesus Christ (Ephesians 5:19-20).

...I will pray with my spirit, but I will also pray with my mind; I will sing with my spirit, but I will also sing with my mind (1 Corinthians 14:15).

Tehillah is song that publicly lauds God both as the praise of Israel and as the One to be praised (see Deut. 10:21; 1 Chron. 16:35; Ps. 22:3; 148:14; Jer. 17:14). Therefore, *tehillah* praise may occur when God's people are praising Him, giving Him praise, or speaking of His praise (see 1 Chron. 16:35; 2 Chron. 20:22; Neh. 12:46; Ps. 22:25; 71:8). In addition, the Scriptures tell us that *tehillah* is praise God is not willing to share with anyone or anything else (see Is. 42:8; Jer. 48:2). It is for Him alone, being the very place of His dwelling (see Ps. 22:3). So zealous is God for the *tehillah* praise of His people, that He even holds back His anger so

He can receive praise (see Is. 48:9). Moreover, the Scriptures tell us that God will make Jerusalem the praise of the earth (see Is. 62:7; Jer. 33:9) as He makes His people praiseworthy (see Deut. 26:19; Zeph. 3:19-20). Then His people themselves will be His praise (see Jer. 33:11).

Nehemiah 9:5 is an interesting usage of this word, in that God's name is "exalted above all blessing [*shabach*] and praise [*tehillah*]." In other words, God is exalted above any praise we can offer Him. Thus it not surprising that *tehillah* is also translated "glory" (see Ex. 15:11).

The Pairing or Progression of the Dimensions in Scripture

Now that we've looked at the meanings of these seven dimensions or portraits of praise, let's look at how they are grouped together. Although they do not occur in the Scriptures in a strict order, or even all in the same praise experience, there is a sense in which one builds upon the other as the worshiper is caught up into seeking the presence of God. At first, there is the verbal thanksgiving for what God has done (*todah*). This usually recounts specific ways the Lord has protected or blessed the worshiper. Then, as the praise becomes more spontaneous, outbursts of thanksgiving combined with the extension of the hands to God in adoration may occur (*yadah*). As the worshiper continues to thank God for personal blessings, a more general honoring and adoring of God may follow (*halal*). This in turn may progress into the making of music (*zamar*) and into expressions of victory and celebration, often with dance. This heightened exhilaration may lessen at times as the worshiper waits with expectancy for God to lead in a new direction or to reveal Himself in some manner (*barak*). Thus, as the intensity of praise ebbs and flows, the worshiper may slip back and forth among the various dimensions of praise.

If we examine the grouping of these seven dimensions in the Scriptures more closely, we find that the pairing of these portraits of praise is quite common, although rarely is the pairing with successive dimensions.

> I will give You thanks [*yadah*] in the great assembly; among throngs of people I will praise [*halal*] You (Psalm 35:18).

> Praise [*barak*] our God, O peoples, let the sound of His praise [*tehillah*] be heard (Psalm 66:8).

Rather, the pairing is more likely to skip a dimension or two.

> Sing to the Lord with thanksgiving [*todah*]; make music [*zamar*] to our God on the harp (Psalm 147:7).

> I will praise [*yadah*] You, O Lord, among the nations; I will sing [*zamar*] of You among the peoples (Psalm 57:9).

> It is good to praise [*yadah*] the Lord and make music [*zamar*] to Your name, O Most High (Psalm 92:1).

> All You have made will praise [*yadah*] You, O Lord; Your saints will extol [*barak*] You (Psalm 145:10).

> Then we Your people, the sheep of Your pasture, will praise [*yadah*] You forever; from generation to generation we will recount Your praise [*tehillah*] (Psalm 79:13).

> Praise [*halal*] the Lord. Sing to the Lord a new song, His praise [*tehillah*] in the assembly of the saints (Psalm 149:1).

> Praise [*halal*] the Lord, for the Lord is good; sing praise [*zamar*] to His name, for that is pleasant (Psalm 135:3).

In addition, these pairings place the various aspects of praise in varying orders that differ from the indicated sequence, with praise moving back and forth between the dimensions.

> Let them give thanks [*yadah*] to the Lord for His unfailing love and His wonderful deeds for men. Let them

sacrifice thank offerings [*todah*] **and tell of His works with songs of joy (Psalm 107:21-22).**

That my heart may sing [*zamar*] to You and not be silent. O Lord my God, I will give You thanks [*yadah*] forever (Psalm 30:12).

I will praise [*halal*] God's name in song and glorify Him with thanksgiving [*todah*] (Psalm 69:30).

The trumpeters and singers joined in unison, as with one voice, to give praise [*halal*] and thanks [*yadah*] to the Lord. Accompanied by trumpets, cymbals and other instruments, they raised their voices in praise [*halal*] to the Lord and sang: "He is good; His love endures forever." Then the temple of the Lord was filled with a cloud (2 Chronicles 5:13).

My mouth will speak in praise [*tehillah*] of the Lord. Let every creature praise [*barak*] His holy name for ever and ever (Psalm 145:21).

Expressions of praise that include three or four dimensions are also present in the Bible, although they are not as common as the pairings.

Cry out, "Save us, O God our Savior; gather us and deliver us from the nations, that we may give thanks [*yadah*] to Your holy name, that we may glory [*shabach*] in Your praise [*tehillah*]" (1 Chronicles 16:35; see also Psalm 106:47).

Praise [*halal*] the Lord. How good it is to sing praises [*zamar*] to our God, how pleasant and fitting to praise [*tehillah*] Him! (Psalm 147:1)

In these instances as well, the praise dimensions may not follow the order noted above.

Enter into His gates with thanksgiving [*todah*], and into His courts with praise [*tehillah*]: be thankful [*yadah*] unto Him, and bless [*barak*] His name (Psalm 100:4 KJV).

A good example of progression through the dimensions of praise is found in First Chronicles chapter 16 when King David takes the Ark of the Covenant to Jerusalem.

They brought the ark of God and set it inside the tent that David had pitched for it, and they presented burnt offerings and fellowship offerings before God. After David had finished sacrificing the burnt offerings and fellowship offerings, he blessed the people in the name of the Lord....He appointed some of the Levites to minister before the ark of the Lord, to make petition, to give thanks [*yadah*], and to praise [*halal*] the Lord, the God of Israel.

That day David first committed to Asaph and his associates this psalm of thanks [*yadah*] to the Lord: Give thanks [*yadah*] to the Lord, call on His name; make known among the nations what He has done. Sing to Him, sing praise to Him; tell of all His wonderful acts. Glory in His holy name; let the hearts of those who seek the Lord rejoice. Look to the Lord and His strength; seek His face always. Remember the wonders He has done, His miracles, and the judgments He pronounced.

Sing to the Lord, all the earth; proclaim His salvation day after day. Declare His glory among the nations, His marvelous deeds among all peoples. For great is the Lord and most worthy of praise [*halal*]; He is to be feared above all gods. For all the gods of the nations are idols, but the Lord made the heavens. Splendor and majesty are before Him; strength and joy in His dwelling place. Ascribe to the Lord, O families of nations, ascribe to the Lord glory and strength, ascribe

> to the Lord the glory due His name. Bring an offering
> and come before Him; worship the Lord in the splendor
> of His holiness....Give thanks [*yadah*] to the Lord, for
> He is good; His love endures forever. Cry out, "Save us,
> O God our Savior; gather us and deliver us from the
> nations, that we may give thanks [yadah] to Your holy
> name, that we may glory [*shabach*] in Your praise [*tehil-*
> *lah*]." Praise [*barak*] be to the Lord, the God of Israel,
> from everlasting to everlasting. Then all the people said
> "Amen" and "Praise [*halal*] the Lord" (1 Chronicles
> 16:1-2,4,7-12,23-29,34-36).

To understand the significance of this passage concerning
praise, we need to go back a chapter and look at the bringing of
the Ark to Jerusalem in chapter 15. David has made a tent for the
Ark of the Covenant and is preparing to bring it into the city.
Therefore, he assembles all the people, including the Levites, the
only Israelites who are permitted to carry the Ark. Then he
instructs them:

> ...You are the heads of the Levitical families; you and
> your fellow Levites are to consecrate yourselves and
> bring up the ark of the Lord, the God of Israel, to the
> place I have prepared for it. It was because you, the
> Levites, did not bring it up the first time that the Lord
> our God broke out in anger against us. We did not
> inquire of Him about how to do it *in the prescribed way*
> (1 Chronicles 15:12-13, emphasis added).

Do you remember what David is talking about here? He had
tried to bring the Ark to Jerusalem before, but tragedy struck
when Uzzah, one of the men taking care of the Ark, was killed
when he put out his hand to steady it (see 1 Chron. 13). Hence,
David's joy in bringing the Ark to Jerusalem was replaced by fear.

David evidently saw this calamity as the result of his failure to
ask God for His prescribed way to move the Ark. The second time

he attempted to move it, he therefore wanted to be sure he did everything right. Instead of placing the Ark on a cart, as he had done the first time, David instructed the Levites to carry it on poles as their ancestors had done in the time of Moses.

As they started out, David commanded the Levites to sing joyful songs, accompanied by musical instruments. David also offered sacrifices to God because He was helping the Levites to move the Ark, as He required. Thus, all Israel brought up the Ark with shouting, rejoicing, and the playing of trumpets and other instruments.

Meanwhile, King David was dancing and celebrating. This lover of God's presence was evidently overjoyed that the throne of God was coming to Jerusalem, the city where David lived and ruled. As we pick up the story in First Chronicles chapter 16, we see that David offers more sacrifices and appoints Levites to minister before the Ark, making petitions, giving thanks (*yadah*), and praising God (*halal*).

David had experienced one tragedy because he didn't follow God's instructions. He wasn't about to suffer another one. Therefore, he instructed the Levites to minister to the Lord starting with sacrifices and thanksgiving. Only after the sacrifices had been presented, did he add music and progress through the other dimensions of praise. Finally, by the end of verse 35, the praise becomes *tehillah*. This progression of praise dimensions is not found here in strict order, as is evident in the verses quoted above. Yet, there is a sense in which David sought to follow God's pattern so the people might "give thanks [*yadah*] to [His] holy name, [and] glory [*shabach*] in [His] praise [*tehillah*]."

Taking a Drink or Going for a Swim

This pattern in praise has not changed. God still requires that we approach Him with sacrifices before we seek His favor and blessing. This is why *tehillah* is the last dimension of praise, not the first. God is not willing to be enthroned among us until He sees that we want *Him*, not just the things He can give us.

> **But Thou art holy, O Thou that inhabitest the praises of Israel** (Psalm 22:3 KJV).

> **Yet You are enthroned as the Holy One; You are the praise of Israel** (Psalm 22:3).

In essence, not just any praise brings God's presence to us. Only praise that follows His pattern, starting with the sacrifices of a willing heart and a contrite spirit and continuing as we quiet ourselves before Him until we yield ourselves completely to Him, will do. Our hearts must be totally consumed with Him, and only Him, as His Spirit reigns supreme in our spirit. This is when God becomes enthroned in our praise and the songs of the spirit begin.

This is not to say that we do not have the Spirit in us before we reach *tehillah* praise. Certainly, we all receive Him when we accept Jesus as Savior. Yet, we may be born again and still not experience the manifest presence of the Lord.

I know this is difficult for some of you to understand, but it is essential that you do, so that God's presence may be a consistent ongoing part of your life. If I describe it this way, perhaps it will help you to understand what I mean: When you are born again, it is like drinking a glass of water. You have water on the inside but not on the outside. On the other hand, when you come to God through *tehillah* praise and He sets up His throne in your presence, it is as though you have climbed into a pool and are surrounded by water.

When you drink water, you do not float. When you drink water, you cannot swim. When you drink water, you still have weight. When you dive into a pool, you are held up by the water and the heaviness is taken away. Therefore, it is easier to move around in a pool than on land.

This is the difference between having God's presence and being in God's presence. You can be saved and still walk around carrying a lot of weight because you never get into God's presence.

When you have God's presence, it quenches your thirst. When you live in His presence, He takes over your whole life.

God wants you to do more than take a drink. He wants you to come into the pool so He can take the weight off your life and you can float. Not all the heavy things you carry with you are relieved when you take a drink of God. They fall off only when the water of God surrounds you and lifts you up. This is where *tehillah* praise takes you. When you put on this garment of praise, the spirit of heaviness lifts and you are free to enjoy life and the sweetness of God's presence day after day.

God comes to us when we follow His pattern.

❖ **PRINCIPLES** ❖

1. Praise that reaches God follows a pattern or progression.

2. This pattern, although it does not follow a strict order, may be seen in seven Hebrew words used to describe the various dimensions or portraits of praise. They are,

   - *Todah*: sacrifices of thanksgiving

   - *Yadah*: thanksgiving with hands extended in adoration

   - *Halal*: praising with abandon

   - *Shabach*: shouting with a sense of triumph

   - *Zamar*: making music

   - *Barak*: blessing God

   - *Tehillah*: singing spiritual songs

3. Praise starts with the sacrifices of a willing heart and a contrite spirit.

Chapter 10

Qualified to Be in God's Presence

Sincerity is no substitution for purity.

God comes to those who meet His conditions. He doesn't come because we want Him to come. Perhaps this is why so many Christians never experience the reality of God's manifest presence. They truly want Him to come but they have no idea what qualifies them to receive this awesome gift.

Yes, God responds to our desire for Him, but our desire must be shown in ways that meet His standards. We must be holy, as He is holy.

As we saw in Chapter 3, God's holiness means that He is pure in motive. He is integrated in His thoughts, words, and actions. He cannot lie; neither can He pretend. Those who want to live in His presence must be as He is.

Obviously, this is not our state apart from God. The father of lies (see Jn. 8:44) has deceived us into rejecting God's truth and accepting his falsehoods. The only way this can change—that is, we see satan's lies for what they are and accept God's word as truth—is if God's holiness rubs off on us as we spend time with Him. In other words, we become holy by associating with Holiness.

Therefore, the whole purpose of God's detailed commands concerning the Tabernacle and the Temple was to provide a way for His people to associate with Him without being destroyed because of their sin. In essence, the rituals of the priests and the people were the means by which man fulfilled God's requirements for coming into His presence. When they did it right, God rewarded them, appearing to the priest between the cherubim in the inner sanctuary and to the nation in smoke or a cloud.

Consecrate Yourselves

Coming into God's presence is not something to be done casually. This is why the command "consecrate yourselves" was a constant refrain in the Old Testament. God demanded that His people cleanse themselves from sin before they came into His presence. For the ancient Hebrews, this meant a series of ritual washings of themselves and their garments, both for the people and the priests (see Ex. 19:10,22). Consecration in preparation for serving God or meeting with Him also meant that the priests were to wear certain clothes and symbols and to present prescribed sacrifices (see Ex. 29–30; 39–40; Lev. 8). Priests and common folks alike were also obligated, as part of their rituals and rules concerning consecration, not to eat unclean food or to touch anything that was unclean according to God's definitions (see Lev. 11). To touch these things made a person unfit to gather with God's people as they stood in His presence. Each rule and regulation concerning the work and worship of God's people, both within the Tabernacle and within their everyday lives, was thus prescribed so that they could be holy in God's sight.

Consecrate yourselves and be holy, because I am the Lord your God. Keep My decrees and follow them. I am the Lord, who makes you holy (Leviticus 20:7-8).

Jesus makes it clear, however, that uncleanness on the outside is not the only form of impurity. In fact, it isn't the most important source of contamination. Rather, uncleanness of heart is what pollutes our lives.

Listen to Me, everyone, and understand this. Nothing outside a man can make him "unclean" by going into him. Rather, it is what comes out of a man that makes him "unclean."...Don't you see that nothing that enters a man from the outside can make him "unclean"? For it doesn't go into his heart but into his stomach, and then out of his body....What comes out of a man is what makes him "unclean." For from within, out of men's hearts, come evil thoughts, sexual immorality, theft, murder, adultery, greed, malice, deceit, lewdness, envy, slander, arrogance and folly. All these evils come from inside and make a man "unclean" (Mark 7:14b-23).

Truth and Purity

Coming to God with praise requires that we cleanse our heart from all the evil that has taken up residence there. This is the message of Psalm 15. What is in our heart matters most of all because this is where truth and righteousness, or lies and unrighteousness, start.

Lord, who may dwell in Your sanctuary? Who may live on Your holy hill? He whose walk is blameless and who does what is righteous, who speaks the truth from his heart and has no slander on his tongue, who does his neighbor no wrong and casts no slur on his fellowman, who despises a vile man but honors those who fear the Lord, who keeps his oath even when it hurts, who lends

his money without usury and does not accept a bribe against the innocent. He who does these things will never be shaken (Psalm 15:1-5).

Truth is at the core of the requirements presented in this Psalm—truth with God and truth with our fellowman. What is in our heart and what we do and say must match. We can't say one thing in public and another in private. We can't act one way in worship on Sunday morning and another way throughout the week in our homes and at our jobs. Righteous integration in all our life is evidently essential if we want God's presence to come and stay with us.

This requirement of inner purity is also evident in Psalms 24 and 101:

Who may ascend the hill of the Lord? Who may stand in His holy place? He who has clean hands and a pure heart, who does not lift up his soul to an idol or swear by what is false. He will receive blessing from the Lord and vindication from God his Savior. Such is the generation of those who seek Him, who seek Your face, O God of Jacob. Selah (Psalm 24:3-6).

No one who practices deceit will dwell in My house; no one who speaks falsely will stand in My presence (Psalm 101:7).

Clean hands, a pure heart, and truth in the innermost being: These are the distinguishing characteristics of the man or woman who may stand in God's presence and offer praise in which God is enthroned.

Jesus evidently agreed with this assessment, for He said that the pure in heart would see God (see Mt. 5:8). He also told the Samaritan woman whom He met at a well,

Yet a time is coming and has now come when the true worshipers will worship the Father in spirit and truth,

for they are the kind of worshipers the Father seeks. God is spirit, and His worshipers must worship in spirit and in truth (John 4:23-24).

Purity and truth in our heart are thus the critical factors that determine whether our praise is acceptable to God. If the form and timing of our praise is right but our heart is not, we cannot expect to receive the gift of His presence.

God Comes When We Truly Want Him

The point I am making is that you don't get God's presence just because you ask for it. You get His presence when you qualify for it. Yes, the torn veil in the Temple because of the death of our Lord Jesus Christ now gives us direct access to the throne of God that the Israelites did not have. And yes, the way is open to all. Yet, we too must ascend into God's presence, climbing the hill of the Lord much as the people of the Old Testament climbed Mount Zion on their way to the Temple.

God wants honest, pure, and committed worshipers. These are His standards for those who would approach Him through praise. Consequently, just any praise will not bring Him to us. Goosepimples and warm fuzzies won't do it. Neither will praise that is concerned more with what we can get from God than with who He is. Our praise must be *tehillah*: praise that has no ulterior motives; praise that comes from a heart cleansed from sin and wholly yielded to and controlled by Him; praise that acknowledges the reality of God, not the creation of God; praise that is wholly focused on Him and the glory of His name. This, I believe, is what Jesus meant when He said,

> **...I tell you the truth, unless you change and become like little children, you will never enter the kingdom of heaven** (Matthew 18:3).

Have you ever watched a child praise and worship? Children are pure in praise. They have nothing else on their mind. Therefore, when they sing, "This is my story, this is my song..." they mean what they say in all simplicity. Older people, on the other hand, are often so busy trying to perform, and worrying about what they sound and look like, that God is completely absent from their thoughts. Both groups are singing the same song, but they have two different mentalities, two distinct attitudes. One is pure; the other is contaminated by division of thought.

This is why we are so captivated by watching young children worship. Their heart is so turned toward God that His anointing comes upon them and they become one with Him. Nothing stands between the praiser and the One being praised, so He comes and reveals Himself in and through them.

God wants this praise from all His people. He wants our love for Him and our praise to be like that of children who come to us, hug us, and say, "I like you." In such moments, we know their love is real. They aren't considering how they can use us to get something or how they can make us love them. When they say, "I love you," this is all they are thinking about and all they mean. There is no plotting going on in their young mind and no hidden motives.

Oh, if we adults could relearn how to welcome God like children do. Now, I am not speaking of being childish. I am talking about being childlike—that is, as little children who are pure in thought, motive, and act. This praise stills the enemy of our souls:

From the lips of children and infants You have ordained praise because of Your enemies, to silence the foe and the avenger (Psalm 8:2).

Most of the time when we adults come to God and say, "I love You," we have this long list in the back of our mind that we want Him to fulfill. Or we are worrying about our families, or about the mortgage, the car payment, or some other bill. We aren't really focusing on God. He is not our heart's true desire. Instead, we are trying to get Him to give us what we want. This is not pure praise because we are not approaching God in truth.

God looks through the crowds who come to church on a Sunday morning for a few who are totally given to Him in their praise. Many come to praise Him, and there may be singing, dancing, and noise everywhere, but few Christians are true worshipers. These devoted ones refuse to be distracted by the events of this morning, yesterday, or last week. They are not concerned with what dress the woman beside them is wearing or what kind of haircut the teenager five rows up has. Their focus is totally on God, and He is their delight.

In essence, God doesn't want you to be thinking about anything or anyone else when you say, "I love You." Nor does He want you to come to Him only when you have a long list of needs and wishes. When you do this, He stays away because He knows that you don't really want Him. You only want what you think you can get from Him.

God is holy—that is, He is pure in thought, motive, and attitude—and He expects you to be holy too. Consequently, don't tell Him something unless you really mean it. He is not pleased when you do something on the outside that doesn't match what you think or feel on the inside. If you sing, "Let us lift up holy hands," but your hands are down at your side, or "Clap your hands all ye people," and you aren't clapping, God isn't going to show up. He recognizes that your mouth is saying one thing but your body is doing another because the impurity of your heart is showing. You don't really mean what you are singing. You are saying the right words, but your heart is not at one with your mouth.

God is seeking true worshipers. He wants your praise on the outside to match what is inside your heart because then your spirit is doing what God's Spirit is telling it to do. You are letting God's holiness rub off on you. This is why Jesus said that true worshipers would worship His Father not only in truth, but also in spirit (see Jn. 4:23-24).

God isn't looking for you to have a Holy Ghost fit. Screaming, jerking, and falling on the ground do not mean that you are worshiping God in spirit. They may mean that you are having an emotional fit. God doesn't want you to have a particular feeling. He's examining your spiritual attitude.

Please be sure you understand this. The word *spirit* in John 4:23-24 is spelled with a lowercase "s," not an uppercase one. In other words, Jesus wasn't talking about the Holy Spirit, but about your spirit. He was saying that the time would come when people would fix up their spirit before they came into His presence. They would get their life in order.

Worship is intercourse with God, and He isn't willing to be contaminated by the junk in your spirit. Therefore, He requires that you clean up your life before He comes to live with you. Once you have purified your attitudes, priorities, and motives, He can believe what you say to Him in praise. He can trust that you are really blessing Him when you say, "Bless the Lord" or "Glory to God."

In spirit and in truth is the bottom line for praise and worship because you can't fool God by trying to fake something that isn't in your heart. True praise requires integrity of heart and humility of spirit that are not easily attained. Those who persevere, however, receive the high prize of God's favor and God's presence.

> **This is the one I esteem: he who is humble and contrite in spirit, and trembles at My word** (Isaiah 66:2b).

> **In my integrity You uphold me and set me in Your presence forever** (Ps. 41:12).

So, check yourself when you come to God. Be sure that what you are saying or doing is in agreement with your heart and spirit. Otherwise, you are wasting your time because God comes only to those who are qualified to enter His presence. These are the people He permits to worship Him.

Worship is the privilege of those who seek God with clean hands and a pure heart.

❖ PRINCIPLES ❖

1. God is integrated in thought, word, and action.

2. God's holiness rubs off on us as we spend time with Him.

3. Uncleanness of heart pollutes our life.

4. Truth with God and our fellowman is required of those who want God to come and stay.

5. Cleaning up our heart prepares us to worship God.

6. God is seeking true worshipers whose words and actions match their heart.

7. *Tehillah* praise permits no thought other than God.

Chapter 11

The Relationship of Praise & Worship

**Praise is seeking God.
Worship is being found by Him.**

The goal of praise is to create an atmosphere for the presence of God. This is why Abraham, Moses, and David were such close friends with God. They made room for Him in their life. Their deep hunger to know and obey Him was the basis for their relationship with Him.

This is true for all genuine worshipers. They love to be with God and He loves to be with them. He shows up because they have an authentic devotion to Him and a passion for Him.

Thus, praise and worship are related but very different activities and experiences.

- Praise is initiated by us. Worship is God's response.

- Praise is something we do. Worship is something God releases.

- Praise is our building a house for God. Worship is God moving in.

Worship cannot be generated by us. It is completely dependent on God. We may seek to enter worship through praise, but it is up to God whether He will respond to our initiative.

In truth, we cannot worship God unless we have first praised Him, and this praise must be genuine. Otherwise, Jesus' indictment against the Pharisees may also be leveled against us:

> **These people honor Me with their lips, but their hearts are far from Me. They worship Me in vain...** (Matthew 15:8-9).

True praise and worship are tough, but the results are awesome because everything we need is in God's presence. Joy, rest, peace, mercy, power, victory, wisdom: All these and more are available to us in the presence of God.

> **You have made known to me the path of life; You will fill me with joy in Your presence, with eternal pleasures at Your right hand** (Psalm 16:11).

> **Surely You have granted him eternal blessings and made him glad with the joy of Your presence** (Psalm 21:6).

> **In the shelter of Your presence You hide them from the intrigues of men; in Your dwelling You keep them safe from accusing tongues** (Psalm 31:20).

These gifts of God's presence are not to be the focus of our search, however. Seeking the blessings of God instead of the face of God never works. When we persist in this, asking God for stuff instead of Himself, we forfeit precisely what we seek. That is, we lose the things we ask for because we fail to gain the presence of the One who holds them in His hand. Then He says to us, "You've missed the most important thing. Seek My Kingdom first. Then I'll give you all the land, houses, food, clothes, and jobs you need." (See Matthew 6:33.)

> **W**e forfeit the things we ask God for when we fail to seek Him first.

Yes, you may find that seeking God first is difficult because your wants and needs clamor for attention. Nevertheless, you must persevere. He knows that you come to Him with many problems, burdens, and questions. He understands your need. Yet, He enjoins you to seek His face before you seek His hand. You may think you need a prayer line, but He knows that you really need time with Him. When He gets into your life, He will fix in one moment things you have been working on for days, weeks, and even years. In this respect, seeking God is quite like praising Him. Your focus must be on Him, and He must be your delight.

Praise Me; Seek Me...With All Your Heart

God responds to people who have a deep hunger for Him.

As the deer pants for streams of water, so my soul pants for You, O God. My soul thirsts for God, for the living God. When can I go and meet with God? (Psalm 42:1-2)

This heart cry of David is the entreaty of every true worshiper. Where is God? Why can't I find Him? How can I build a road to where He is so that I may be with Him?

So deep is the hunger and thirst of these committed ones that they seek God until they are caught by Him. Their passion for Him will not allow them to stop until they gain the One for whom they reach. Hours spent in prayer and praise are the rule for them, not the exception.

This attitude is uncommon in the Church. We are much too comfortable to expend the effort such a passion requires. Why is this? Why are we so lackadaisical in our search for God? One possible answer is that we have yet to experience the beauty and power of God's manifest presence. Therefore, we don't understand that the reward for our seeking is worth every bit of our effort, and more.

Another possibility is that our self-centeredness and the competing loyalties within us prevent us from giving full allegiance to anyone, including God. We cannot seek Him with all our heart because there are too many closed doors in us that bar God from entering.

Walking in God's ways and obeying Him in all things is a privilege, not a hindrance. Yet we often treat God as such. When things become a little difficult—we don't like singing choruses, we are out too late Saturday night, we begin to tire from standing during the praise and worship time—we are quick to assume that coming to church and giving God our full attention is an imposition rather than a blessing. How wrong we are!

Remember that God doesn't need us so that He can be God. We need Him so that we can be human. Seeking Him is for our benefit, not His. When we praise and seek God, He turns around and finds us. He gives us Himself, which is all we really need.

If, then, we find that we are unable to seek God because of the many obstacles in our life, what are we to do? Get rid of the junk and clean house.

> **When we praise and seek God, He turns around and finds us.**

Praise Me; Seek Me...With Repentance

As the children of Israel were about to enter the Promised Land, Joshua recounted all that God had done for them and challenged them to choose whom they would serve.

> But if serving the Lord seems undesirable to you, then choose for yourselves this day whom you will serve...But as for me and my household, we will serve the Lord (Joshua 24:15).

The people chose to serve God.

> Far be it from us to forsake the Lord to serve other gods! It was the Lord our God Himself who brought us and our fathers up out of Egypt, from that land of slavery, and performed those great signs before our eyes....We too will serve the Lord, because He is our God (Joshua 24:16b-18).

Then Joshua charged them, "Throw away the foreign gods that are among you and yield your hearts to the Lord, the God of Israel" (Josh. 24:23b). In other words, he told them to make themselves qualified for serving God.

Seeking God is always this way. We cannot keep the idols of our heart and expect to receive the gift of His presence. Repentance is, therefore, an essential ingredient of seeking and praising Him. We must return to Him on a daily basis so He can turn to us. In essence, His coming to us is predicated on the fact that we get rid of all the obstacles that keep us from coming to Him.

Praise Me; Seek Me...With Humility and Trust

Unfortunately, getting rid of everything in our life that keeps us from God is an arduous task that none of us can complete. Frankly, we are not capable of it. We need God to do it for us. Yet, He cannot free us from all that entangles us unless we are willing to let Him take over our life. Most of us find this easier to say than do. Very often we hand Him the reins one day and take them back the next. Perhaps we do this because we have not learned a truth that was quite precious to David:

> **Those who know Your name will trust in You, for You, Lord, have never forsaken those who seek You** (Psalm 9:10).

Trust is a necessity if we are to genuinely seek and praise the Lord. Otherwise, we will take matters into our own hands when we don't like what is happening in our life or we don't understand the path God has set before us. David could have done this many times in the years between when he was anointed king by Samuel and when he was enthroned by the people. In fact, his trust in God was repeatedly tested.

On one occasion when he was running from King Saul, who sought him to kill him, David had the opportunity to kill Saul. From a human perspective, this certainly would have advanced David's cause. Yet, David, because He believed in God's faithfulness to him, chose to wait for God's timing instead of taking things into his own hands.

> **The Lord rewards every man for his righteousness and faithfulness. The Lord delivered you** [King Saul] **into my hands today, but I would not lay a hand on the Lord's anointed. As surely as I valued your life today, so may the Lord value my life and deliver me from all trouble** (1 Samuel 26:23-24).

God is searching for such a generation, a people who will value His presence over their own selfish desires and wait for His purposes despite long periods of preparation. Such a generation will approach Him with humility, subjecting their pride-filled hearts to the searching of His eyes. They will value Him and His plans for them above all else.

> **The Lord looks down from heaven on the sons of men to see if there are any who understand, any who seek God** (Psalm 14:2).

These people will be caught by God, for His plans and purposes always include intimacy with Him.

I love those who love Me, and those who seek Me find Me (Proverbs 8:17).

They also include a future that is much brighter than any of us can imagine.

"For I know the plans I have for you," declares the Lord, "plans to prosper you and not to harm you, plans to give you hope and a future. Then you will call upon Me and come and pray to Me, and I will listen to you. You will seek Me and find Me when you seek Me with all your heart. I will be found by you," declares the Lord... (Jeremiah 29:11-14).

When people genuinely want God's presence, He gives it to them. This is the bottom line of praise and worship. Hence, David instructed his son Solomon to continue as he had started.

And you, my son Solomon, acknowledge the God of your father, and serve Him with wholehearted devotion and with a willing mind, for the Lord searches every heart and understands every motive behind the thoughts. If you seek Him, He will be found by you; but if you forsake Him, He will reject you forever (1 Chronicles 28:9).

The same challenge comes to you. Choose to be an Abraham, Joseph, Moses, David, or Daniel. Praise and seek God with all your heart. Then wait and see what He will do in your life. I promise you that He will fulfill His ultimate goal and desire for you: He will grace you with His presence.

Worship: The Climax of Praise

Worship is what praise is all about: Seeking God until He graces us with His presence. Once He is present, everybody and everything else is dismissed. The prophet Habukkuk referred to this when he said,

> **...the Lord is in His holy temple; let all the earth be silent before Him** (Habukkuk 2:20).

When God shows up, everybody else has to shut up. This is illustrated quite well in Second Chronicles chapter 5, which describes the dedication of Solomon's Temple.

The dedication was preceded by the transfer of the Ark of the Covenant to the inner sanctuary of the Temple, where it was placed beneath the wings of the cherubim. More sacrifices than could be counted accompanied this event. Then the priests withdrew from the Holy Place and consecrated themselves so they would be holy in their relationship to God.

After this, the Levites, who were dressed in fine linen, began to make music unto the Lord with cymbals, harps, and lyres, and they were accompanied by 120 priests playing trumpets. In addition, singers raised their voices with the instruments to give praise and thanks to the Lord. This was some choir and some orchestra. Their praise must have literally filled the Holy Place and spilled beyond to the Outer Court as they sang: "He is good; His love endures forever" (see 2 Chron. 5:13).

Now watch what happens:

> **Then the temple of the Lord was filled with a cloud, and the priests could not perform their service because of the cloud, for the glory of the Lord filled the temple of God** (2 Chronicles 5:13b-14).

Please try to get a picture of this in your mind. Sacrifices and thanksgiving were offered as the Ark of the Covenant was taken into the Temple. Then the priests consecrated themselves in preparation for the service of dedication. As this time of praise began, the orchestra played first. Then the trumpeters and singers joined in. Finally, after all the sacrifices, thanksgiving, and unified offerings of praise, the power of God came into the Temple so strong that the priests could not stand up! In truth, everyone in the place was flattened like a line of dominoes. They couldn't perform their duties because the cloud of God's glory filled the place.

Finding God and enjoying His presence is the sole purpose of our praise. Only then may we know what to do and how to live effectively. God is raising up a praising Body all over the world. He's preparing a generation who will seek Him above all else. When they start singing, governments are going to become afraid. When they start shouting, nations all around the world are going to be transformed. Then, when God finally comes and sits in the midst of all this praise, our world is going to see miracle upon miracle as the walls of prejudice, hatred, and division fall. (See Joshua chapter 6.) Indeed, our world will change so fast that we will be hard put to keep up with everything God is doing. This is the power and authority of praise that leads God's people into worship, taking them the whole way into His presence.

> **F**inding and enjoying God is the goal of all praise.

❖ **PRINCIPLES** ❖

1. God responds to people who have a deep hunger for Him.

2. Passionate worshipers love to be with God, and He loves to be with them.

3. Praise and worship are related but different activities:

   • Praise is initiated by us. Worship is God's response.

   • Praise is something we do. Worship is something God releases.

   • Praise is our building a house for God. Worship is God moving in.

4. Repentance is a necessary part of seeking and praising God.

5. Humility and trust free God to reward those who seek Him.

6. God's plans for each person include intimacy with Him and a future filled with hope.

7. When God shows up in the midst of His people, everything else suddenly stops.

Chapter 12

The Power of Praise & Worship

The purpose of praise is to get God into your environment. The power of praise is the presence of God at work in your life.

When God comes, things change. This is not to say that God changes, for He was God long before we were born, and He'll be God long after we die. He was God before anything was created, and He will be God after everything has passed away. God is God, even without us. Therefore, telling God that He is great, beautiful, and all-powerful does not make Him any of these things.

> **P**raise acknowledges the reality of who God already is.

To say it another way, when we praise God, we agree with what He has already said and shown us about who He is. We also discover more of who He created us to be because we were made to be like He is and His presence is the environment He created us to live in. Therefore, holiness is good for us because when we are holy, holiness meets Holiness.

Things also change when God leaves. The life of King Saul shows us what a difference the absence or presence of God can make. Saul had disobeyed God and, therefore, was tormented by an evil spirit. (See First Samuel chapters 13,15–16.) Since no other cure was available, Saul's servants suggested that they find someone to play the harp whenever the spirit came. Saul agreed and David came to play for him. As David skillfully played the songs he wrote, the presence of the Lord filled the room and the evil spirit had to go. When David left, however, the spirit returned, since the presence of God was absent from Saul's life. In essence, Saul had to call for David repeatedly because he did not know how to attract the presence of God through praise.

This must not be true for you. You should not have to come to church or call someone else to get into God's presence. You must practice drawing God to you through praise until His presence is with you every day and all day. Then, no matter where you are and what you are experiencing, you will have the key that opens doors no one can shut, and shuts doors no one can open (see Rev. 3:7).

Consequently, if something is blocking your way, or someone is trying to hold back your blessing, don't get mad or complain. Start praising the Lord. Then He'll show up in your situation and make things right.

God's Presence Brings Joy

When the Lord's presence is in a place with you, it makes you feel so good that you want to hang around for awhile. You don't want to lose the delicious reality you are experiencing. So great is this joy of being with God that you may even do things you normally won't do. For example, you may be nice to everybody, hugging folks you don't even like.

David evidently knew this wonderful feeling because he said,

You have made known to me the path of life; You will fill me with joy in Your presence, with eternal pleasures at Your right hand (Psalm 16:11).

God's presence is the source of joy. If you want to have more joy in your life, spend more time with God. Then the spirit of heaviness that hangs on you will lift as God changes your attitudes and perspectives.

One joy-filled experience in God's presence is all it will take to make you hunger for more. So, refuse to be content where you are. Seek God each day until joy becomes your constant companion and you become as delighted with God's presence as was David, who preferred one day with God to a thousand with an earthly king (see Ps. 84:10).

God's Presence Gives Rest

Rest is also a gift of God's presence. Often we wear ourselves out trying to meet responsibilities in our own strength. Moses did this. When he asked God to give him help with the work of leading the Israelites, God said, "My Presence will go with you..." (Ex. 33:14b). Moses was looking for people to help him: "Give me some assistance, Lord. I need some managers, supervisors, and workers." God gave Moses Himself and the promise of rest.

The word translated here as *rest* means among other things "to settle down," "to give comfort," "to cease," "to be quiet," and "to cause to rest, be at rest, give rest, have rest, make to rest" (Strong's, H5117). The word may also mean "to set one's mind at rest" (Vine's, "To Rest, Remain"). In truth, this rest is a ceasing to work because the work is not ours. When God is with us, He is the

One who does the work, and we are freed from the anxiety of trying to make things right.

Hence, God was saying to Moses, "All you need is My presence. When I am with you, you don't have to work so hard. I will meet all your needs and take care of your concerns."

The Church today needs to understand this principle. We become so caught up in planning and programs that we forget who is in charge of the Church. You and I certainly will not accomplish God's plans; neither will anyone we may find to help in the work. Success comes when God comes. Until then, we are simply spinning our wheels.

God's Presence Brings Peace

The disciples learned this lesson one night on the Sea of Galilee. Jesus had been teaching the crowds and ministering to people all day. As night fell, He said to His disciples, "Let us go over to the other side" (Mk. 4:35b). While they were on the lake, a terrible storm came upon them so that they feared for their lives. Meanwhile Jesus was asleep in the boat. So they woke Him saying, "Teacher, don't You care if we drown?" (vs. 38b) Jesus got up and commanded the wind and waves, "Quiet! Be still!" (vs. 39b), and there was complete calm. Then He said to His disciples, "Why are you so afraid? Do you still have no faith?" (vs. 40b)

The disciples were working hard in that storm. Jesus, on the other hand, said only three short words, "Quiet! Be still!" He didn't have to bail water or shout commands at people. He simply spoke to the wind and the waves, and they obeyed Him.

God's presence in our life brings the same calm and peace. This peace doesn't necessarily mean, however, that everything is quiet. God's peace means that we aren't worrying about anything.

Sometimes we get uptight when things aren't going the way we want or expect. So we rush around and start giving orders until everyone around us is as uptight as we are. Our problem in such situations is that we are trying to deal with our difficulties by ourselves.

God wants you to understand that you don't have to solve your problems. All you must do is get Him in the midst of them. Just start praising Him until His presence starts making a difference in your situation. Then you'll have total prosperity, total quietness in spirit, and total union with God.

Some of you are stressed and depressed today, and you desperately need God's presence. You need His peace and calm in place of the anxiety and struggle you've been going through. Tylenol or an anti-depressant drug won't give you this peace. They cannot fix you. Even if you feel better for a short time, the pills will soon wear off and you will be right back where you were before you took them. Instead of reaching for pills, reach for Jesus. Pills just deal with the symptoms of the problem. God deals with the root. When His presence is in your house, your struggle and anxiety are replaced with His peace and rest.

So stop reading for a few moments and lift your hands right now to God. Praise Him for the good things He has brought into your life. I know you may not feel like praising Him, but now is the time to make your will take control over your emotions. Thank Him for the gift of peace He has for you. Thank Him that He is in control of your life. Thank Him for His concern for you and His never-ending faithfulness to you. Thank Him that He'll never leave you or forsake you. Just bring Him this sacrifice of praise until you sense His presence in your spirit. Then bask in His love and His tender care for you.

We worry so much because we think that we have to fix everything. God is the one who fixes things, not us. Our responsibility is to make the conditions right so He can come and do His work. When we make room for Him through praise, He comes in and takes over.

This is why protecting God's presence in our life is absolutely essential. In essence, we are protecting ourselves by making room for Him. As soon as we become aware of anything that is disrupting His presence, be that in our personal life or in our life together as God's people, we must activate praise and take charge over whatever is threatening us. Our peace of mind demands this. As we fight for God's presence, being zealous to guard it, we will find that our moments of crisis and turmoil become less frequent because God is in our environment all the time to bring us peace.

Without God's presence, we are always looking for help. With His presence, our souls are at rest and our labors are easy. We find true peace by avoiding the struggle before it begins.

Take My yoke upon you and learn from Me, for I am gentle and humble in heart, and you will find rest for your souls (Matthew 11:29).

God's Presence Attracts the Right People

Once we are at peace with what's happening in our lives, we can trust God to bring the right people and the right opportunities our way. In fact, we will find that miracles are more abundant when we stop trying to do everything in our own strength. People are attracted to us because they are attracted to God. Moses evidently knew this:

..."If Your Presence does not go with us, do not send us up from here. How will anyone know that You are pleased with me and with Your people unless You go with us? What else will distinguish me and Your people from all the other people on the face of the earth?" (Exodus 33:15-16)

Your life should be distinguished because God hangs out with you, not for what you have or what you do. When God is with you, people are drawn to you and they don't know why. They see something they can't describe and feel something they can't articulate. They know something is going on with you even if they don't know what. In truth, they are being drawn to God, not to you. His presence with you is what makes the difference.

The contrary is also true. Some folks who come around are attracted more by the things you do and the blessings you have received than by the presence of God. This, again, is why you need the consistent, enduring presence of God. He'll clean your house so that people who aren't supposed to be in your life will leave.

God's Presence Brings Blessings

What are God's blessings, and how do we know when we have received them? To receive the blessings of God is to receive anything and everything you need to fulfill your life. King David put it this way:

> **Blessed are those You choose and bring near to live in Your courts! We are filled with the good things of Your house, of Your holy temple** (Psalm 65:4).

We are tempted to think that the good things of God's house are material things. Although God may certainly bless us with prosperity, the good things of God are the essential qualities of His character: love, joy, peace, patience, kindness, goodness, faithfulness, gentleness, and self-control.

Hence, we can attest to the goodness of God in our life when we start to look and act as He does and to fulfill His purposes for us. This naturally happens when God is Lord over all aspects of our life. It is as if He says, "You praise Me, and I'll praise you. You honor Me, and I'll honor you. You lift Me up, and I'll lift you up." In essence, we bless ourselves when we bless God through praise and worship. David testified to this when he said that those who have clean hands and a pure heart will receive blessings from the Lord. (See Psalm 24:3-5.)

The contrary may also be true. God may remove blessings from our life if we refuse to bless and honor His name. This is what happened to Eli the priest, who was serving God when Samuel was born. When Eli was old, his sons were dishonoring God and taking advantage of the people they were supposed to be serving.

> **Therefore the Lord, the God of Israel, declares: "I promised that your house and your father's house would minister before Me forever." But now the Lord declares: "Far be it from Me! Those who honor Me I will honor, but those who despise Me will be disdained"** (1 Samuel 2:30).

Truly, our obedience in honoring God and our disobedience in treating Him with contempt have lasting consequences!

God's Presence Brings Power

God's power activated in our life through praise and worship has many benefits. In fact, we cannot recount the sum of them. Nor can we fathom the totality of God's power that is available to us. We are simply too shortsighted. Yet, I want to list some of the ways God's power is at work in us and through us, making our life quite different from what it would be without Him.

God's Presence Protects Us and Gives Us Security

> **If you make the Most High your dwelling—even the Lord, who is my refuge—then no harm will befall you, no disaster will come near your tent. For He will command His angels concerning you to guard you in all your ways; they will lift you up in their hands, so that you will not strike your foot against a stone. You will tread upon the lion and the cobra; you will trample the great lion and the serpent. "Because he loves Me," says the Lord, "I will rescue him; I will protect him, for he acknowledges My name. He will call upon Me, and I will answer him; I will be with him in trouble, I will deliver**

him and honor him. With long life will I satisfy him and show him My salvation" (Psalm 91:9-16).

The truth of these words is certainly seen in the stories of Daniel and his Hebrew friends. Do you remember these young men? They were youth when the people of Judah were taken into captivity in Babylon. Despite the hardships of being taken far from home, Daniel and his friends remained true to God in the land of their exile. In fact, when their faith in God and their devotion to Him got them into big trouble with the rulers of the land, they still chose to trust God and obey Him, even though their choice meant death. In the end, their faithfulness to God became a wonderful opportunity for Him to show them and their captors the greatness of His power and the magnitude of His faithfulness to those who trust Him with everything, including their life.

For Daniel, God's presence came to him in a lion's den. (See Daniel chapter 6.) For the other three—Shadrach, Meshach, and Abednego—a fiery furnace was the place of God's visitation. (See Daniel chapter 3.) The place is not important. The faithfulness and power of God are. He is able and willing to meet you in whatever den of lions or blazing furnace you may find yourself, and His power is more than sufficient to preserve you from harm. So, reach out to Him today through praise. Make room for Him to enter the place of your hardship so that you, like these Hebrew youth, may find His presence is sufficient for all your needs.

God Takes Dominion Over Our Environment

We saw in Chapter 6 how God came into the prison with Paul and Silas and took over. A similar thing happened to Peter. Herod had arrested Peter and put him in prison because the Jews were pleased Herod had killed James, the brother of John. Since it was the Feast of Passover, Herod decided to wait until after the feast to deal with Peter. Meanwhile, the Church was earnestly praying for Peter. The night before Peter was to be brought to trial, God sent an angel to him:

> They passed the first and second guards and came to
> the iron gate leading to the city. It opened for them by
> itself, and they went through it. When they had walked
> the length of one street, suddenly the angel left him.
> Then Peter came to himself and said, "Now I know with-
> out a doubt that the Lord sent His angel and rescued
> me...." When this had dawned on him, he went to the
> house of Mary the mother of John, also called Mark,
> where many people had gathered and were praying
> (Acts 12:10-12).

This story differs from God's intervention for Paul and Silas
in that the Scriptures make no mention of Peter praising God
when the angel of the Lord came to him. We are told, however,
that the Church was seeking God on Peter's behalf. In other
words, they were trying to get God's presence into Peter's environment. As the story shows us, they were successful and Peter's
circumstances changed.

The same is true for you. When you bring God into your environment, your circumstances change. In fact, you might be quite
surprised what would happen if God came and lived in your house
and in your neighborhood. Things would change as He took
authority over demons and strongholds that you have been powerless to touch. This is the power of God's presence in your life.

God Disarms Satan

Some of us, however, have a hard time inviting God to be with
us. We are too busy, we become tired or bored, or we fight against
praise that to us seems to be undignified. Do you know why this
happens? The devil is always trying to make us unavailable to God
or uncomfortable in praise and worship. In other words, satan does
all he can to keep God's power and authority from showing up.

He brings distracting thoughts to our mind: "Did I remember
to turn the iron off?" He tries to shame us: "God's not going to
accept you after what you did last night." He makes us ill or gives

us pain, whether physical or emotional. He sends interruptions, like a ringing telephone or a crying child in Sunday worship. In all this, the devil is doing whatever he can to keep our mind on other things and off God. Indeed, the telephone may not ring all day and a child may not cry in worship until the moment you stand before the Lord in praise. Then the telephone rings not once, but three or four times, and the child cannot be hushed.

Praise that leads to worship stops all this because when God's presence comes, the devil must leave. Truly, a praising saint is the devil's worse nightmare. This is why perseverance is called for in such times. You must make the conscious choice to ignore whatever distractions satan sends. When this is not possible, you must deal with the interruption as quickly as possible and return your focus to God. By doing this, you render satan powerless.

This, in part, is what Paul refers to in Second Corinthians,

The weapons we fight with are not the weapons of the world. On the contrary, they have divine power to demolish strongholds (2 Corinthians 10:4).

The weapons of our warfare to overcome the enemy are prayer and praise. This praise is to be not only the hymns we find in books, but the prayers and songs only the Spirit can give.

...I will pray with my spirit, but I will also pray with my mind; I will sing with my spirit, but I will also sing with my mind (1 Corinthians 14:15).

Such praise confuses the enemy. He can't believe that you are praising God while he is coming against you.

Praise in your everyday life protects you by disarming satan before his assault gains momentum. He becomes confused and thinks something is wrong with him because your praise in difficult circumstances makes no sense to him. He can't understand why you are praising God when your business is shutting down, you're losing your job, and you won't have any income for your family. When he expects you to be the most depressed, you are standing before God singing!

This is the power of praise that begins with thanksgiving and takes you into God's presence. You stop the enemy in his tracks and take the spoils of his warfare right from his hands! (See Second Chronicles chapter 20.) Every evil spirit, every disease, every fear, every bout of depression, every seed of bitterness must flee when God's presence comes because He puts our enemies under our feet.

Vindicate Us

The word *vindicate* means, among other things, "to deliver," "to avenge," and "to defend" (Webster's). King David speaks of this triumph over our enemies in Psalm 24 when he says that those who stand in God's presence will receive vindication from God. In other words, David is saying that God retaliates against whatever is attacking us or is making life difficult for us. He frees us from guilt, fear, bitterness, hatred, insecurities...anything and everything that causes us to be ineffective and unable to live as He created us to function.

This was certainly evident in the life of Joseph, the son of Jacob. (See Genesis chapters 37,39–50.) He had every reason to be angry and bitter, yet he chose to look to God, who blessed him.

> **The Lord was with Joseph and he prospered...** (Genesis 39:2).

> **But while Joseph was there in the prison, the Lord was with him; He showed him kindness and granted him favor in the eyes of the prison warden** (Genesis 39:20b-21).

God's Presence Brings Wisdom and Vision

God's presence always blesses us and enables us to do our best. Our trust in Him, born out of an intentional lifestyle of praise, helps us to look beyond the immediate to what He yet will do. In essence, our eyes of faith cause us to praise Him for the victory that is yet unseen. Confusion, on the other hand, is the result of being outside God's presence. No, we may not always see what God is doing and where He is taking us, for I'm sure Joseph had some questions as he went from being the favored son to being a slave and a prisoner. Nevertheless, God's presence gives us the peace to trust Him and to take each step as He reveals it.

Maybe you have a dream that is so big you are running in circles and laying awake at night wondering how you will accomplish it. Please understand that God deliberately made your dream so big you would need Him to fulfill it. He intends that the two of you will work together. So, start praising God. As you hold before Him all He has already done in your life, you give Him the opportunity to do more. You also open the door for Him to give you all the wisdom and knowledge that are found in Him. Suddenly, what in your human sight appeared to be impossible, comes to pass because God is working for you, in you, and through you.

This is why Moses could throw down his staff and it became a snake, and pick it up again and it became his staff (see Ex. 4:2-4). He was in God's presence, and everything God asked of him, He also gave him the power to do.

The same is true for you. God wants to help you accomplish things you never dreamed were possible. Consequently, you must refuse to be like some folks, who are so set in their ways that had they been Moses, they would not have thrown the staff on the ground in the first place. God uses people who are open to Him. He reveals Himself to these believers who long for His presence and readily respond to His leading. When He is ready to do something new, He turns to them. Others may eventually catch on and start to accept the new stuff from God, but praisers and worshipers are the first to do so.

So, if you don't understand something, don't say anything. Just close your mouth and wait until you have more insight into what God is doing. Living in His presence all the time gives you the opportunity to see things from His perspective. In time, He will show you whether what is happening is from Him.

God's Presence Is the Answer to All the Needs of Our World

This need to discern God's leading will be essential until the time of our Lord's return. Those who listen and watch closely will have the privilege of being part of the transformation that even now is taking place.

The Book of Revelation discloses some of what this advancing Kingdom of God entails. The last two chapters, in particular, speak of the new Jerusalem that will come "down out of heaven from God..." (Rev. 21:2b). In this city, God will fulfill His purpose of the ages and will make everything new, returning to His original purpose when He created man:

> **And I heard a loud voice from the throne saying, "Now the dwelling of God is with men, and He will live with them. They will be His people, and God Himself will be with them and be their God" (Revelation 21:3).**

This city will be filled with the nature of God, and the river of the water of life, pure as crystal, will flow from the throne of God and of the Lamb. Beside the river will be planted the tree of life,

> **...bearing twelve crops of fruit, yielding its fruit every month. And the leaves of the tree are for the healing of the nations. No longer will there be any curse. The throne of God and of the Lamb will be in the city, and His servants will serve Him. They will see His face, and His name will be on their foreheads (Revelation 22:2-4).**

Oh, what glory! In this new Jerusalem, God's servants get what Moses asked for: God's presence is continually with them and they see Him face to face!

This is what Jesus meant when He said He was going to prepare a place for us.

And if I go and prepare a place for you, I will come back and take you to be with Me that you also may be where I am (John 14:3).

Notice the tense of the last verb in this verse. Jesus is making a place so that we can be where He *is*. God wants us to enjoy Him now and to be empowered by His presence. He intends that we live with Him today, next week, and forever. This dwelling of God with man is the sole purpose of all His work throughout history. He is getting us back to the environment of His presence so we can be the men and women He designed us to be.

This transformation is to start with the Church. We are to be the place where God's presence resides all the time so people can come to us and find God. In truth, it is our obligation to make a place from which the fragrance of God spills over into the community around us. Therefore, the day is coming, and perhaps already is here, when the Church will leave the confines of our beautiful, comfortable sanctuaries and will go to the cities of our nations, there to sing and worship the Lord. There will be no preaching or conversation, just praise and worship as hundreds of people stand on street corners bringing the presence of God into our cities and neighborhoods. Arguments and words of persuasion will have no place, because we won't be talking to anyone except our wonderful, all-powerful God. Our attention will be focused on Him instead of the people and problems that surround us.

In that hour, the power of God will take over our countries. He'll just move in, confuse the enemy, and declare victory. People will lay down their weapons, give up their dope, get along with their neighbors, and be reconciled to their families without understanding what is happening to them. There'll be no evangel-ists, no invitations, and no prayer lines to draw them in. They'll just fall to their knees right where they are and cry out to God, whose presence has the power to woo them without the interven-tion of man.

Truly, God's presence is the answer to all the needs of every person in our world, and His presence comes to us through praise. The needs of our families will be met if we start praising God in our homes. The problems of our cities will be solved if we fill our streets with praise and worship. The dilemmas that face our nations will be resolved if we infiltrate every branch of government—every session of our legislatures, every case before our courts, and every meeting with our presidents, prime ministers, and other national leaders—with committed Christians who take praise seriously.

God wants the people He created to live in His presence, and in the end He's going to get what He wants. We know this because He has promised it and He cannot lie. He's going to have His presence here on earth among His people.

The question is whether we will do our part to bring His pur-poses to pass. For you see, the coming of His presence here, today, in our world, is dependent on our praising Him. This is what attracts God's presence, and God's presence is the source that sup-plies every need in our world.

Indeed, God will fill our homes, our churches, our factories, our schools, and our government buildings...every place we can imagine...when we fill that same place with praise. Then we will receive all the answers to life's questions because the answers are in God's presence. This is His purpose and He's going to bring it to pass. Hallelujah! Praise the Lord!

❖ **PRINCIPLES** ❖

1. Every place the enemy has taken up residence must be vacated when God enters that place.

2. God's presence brings...

   - joy, peace, and rest;

   - His blessings, and people to help us fulfill the vision He has given us;

   - security and deliverance from everything that causes us to be ineffective in life;

   - changed circumstances and victory over satan;

   - wisdom and the vision to see what He is doing.

3. God's presence is the answer to all the needs of our world.

4. God's final goal is to live continually with His people, where they can see Him face to face.

Bibliography

Buttrick, George Arthur, ed. *The Interpreter's Dictionary of the Bible*. 5 Volumes. New York: Abingdon Press, 1962.

Butler, Trent C. *Holman Bible Dictionary*. Nashville: Holman Bible Publishers, 1991. All rights reserved. International copyright secured. CD-ROM. Quickverse Library. Parsons Technology, 1996.

Merriam Webster's Collegiate Dictionary. Tenth Ed. Springfield, MA: Merriam-Webster, Incorporated, 1994.

Strong, James. *Strong's Exhaustive Concordance of the Bible*. World Bible Publishers, 1980, 1986. All rights reserved. CD-ROM. Quickverse 4.0. Parsons Technology, 1996.

Vine, William Edwy; Unger, Merrill Frederick; and White, William. *Vine's Complete Expository Dictionary of Old and New Testament Words*. One-Volume Edition. New York: Thomas Nelson Publishers, 1985.

Books by Best-Selling Author
Dr. Myles Munroe

Exciting titles
by Dr. Millicent Thompson

━ DON'T DIE IN THE WINTER...

Why do we go through hard times? Why must we suffer pain? In *Don't Die in the Winter...* Dr. Thompson, a pastor, teacher, and conference speaker, explains the spiritual seasons and cycles that people experience. A spiritual winter is simply a season that tests our growth. We need to endure our winters, for in the plan of God, spring always follows winter!
ISBN 1-56043-558-5

━ CRASHING SATAN'S PARTY

Don't let satan hinder the power of God from working in your life any longer! In this book you'll discover the strategies and devices the enemy uses against you. Too many of us attribute our troubles to God when they are really of the devil. The adversary is subtle and delights in deception. We must be able to recognize *who* is doing *what* in our lives so that we can react according to God's Word. Learn how to destroy the works of the enemy. You can crash satan's party and overcome!
ISBN 1-56043-268-3

━ POT LIQUOR

Did you know that you can learn more about life over a "bowl of collard greens and some good conversation" than you can learn on a therapist's couch? Hidden in shared stories and passed-down advice are life lessons that you can learn from without experiencing the pain. Like a full course spiritual meal, *Pot Liquor* is guaranteed to feed your soul and keep you coming back for more!
ISBN 1-56043-301-9

Exciting titles
by Dr. Wanda Davis-Turner

━━ SEX TRAPS

Discover the tactics of the enemy that lead you down the road of unparalleled remorse. Satan's traps are set with a burning desire to birth pain, guilt, and shame in your life. Learn to avoid the traps!
ISBN 1-56043-193-8

Also available as a workbook.
ISBN 1-56043-300-0

━━ I STOOD IN THE FLAMES

If you have ever come to a point of depression, fear, or defeat, then you need this book! With honesty, truth, and clarity, Dr. Davis-Turner shares her hard-won principles for victory in the midst of the fire. You can turn satan's attack into a platform of strength and laughter!
ISBN 1-56043-275-6

VIDEOS FROM DR. WANDA DAVIS-TURNER

━━ GOD'S ORIGINAL PLAN FOR THE FAMILY
ISBN 0-7684-0049-X

━━ PRIVATE DELIVERANCE IN A PUBLIC PLACE
ISBN 0-7684-0054-6

━━ REMEMBER TO FORGET
ISBN 0-7684-0048-1

━━ SEX TRAPS
ISBN 0-7684-0030-9

━━ THE OTHER MIRACLE
ISBN 0-7684-0053-8

Available at your local Christian bookstore.

For more information and sample chapters, visit www.reapernet.com

6B-1:34

Exciting titles
by Don Nori